AF541619

EMPLOYEES AND CREDIT SOCIETIES

EMPLOYEES AND CREDIT SOCIETIES

By

Dr. M. Edwin Gnanadhas, Ph.D

Reader in Commerce
Scott Christian College (Autonomous)
Nagercoil - 629 003
Kanyakumari District

&

Dr. P. Geetha, Ph.D,

Lecturer
Dept. of Commerce
S.T. Hindu College
Nagercoil - 629 002
Kanyakumari District

DISCOVERY PUBLISHING HOUSE PVT. LTD.
NEW DELHI-110 002

First Published-2010

ISBN 978-81-8356-579-0

Published by:

DISCOVERY PUBLISHING HOUSE PVT. LTD.
4831/24, Ansari Road, Prahlad Street
Darya Ganj, New Delhi-110002 (India)
Phone: +91-11-23279245, 43764432 • Fax: +91-11-23253475
E-mail: parul.wasan@gmail.com
info@discoverypublishinggroup.com
web: www.discoverypublishinggroup.com

Printed at:
Arora Offset Press, Delhi – 92

PREFACE

Co-operation as a system and thought plays a vital role in the economic development of a nation. Recognizing the need for finding out the challenges before the co-operatives in this globalised era a thorough study of Employees co-operative thrift and credit societies, the major non agricultural credit societies is carried out and the results are presented in this book.

The analysis part of this study is classified in to three. The first part clearly analyses the financial performance of the societies. Various statistical tools such as compound growth rate annual growth rate, multiple regression and ratio analysis are applied and the results are presented vividly.

The second part of the analysis work is regarding the members-the real owners of the societies. The profile of the members, their problems, their attitude, association between profile and attitude of the members and their suggestions for the improvement of the societies are analysed with the help of the statistical tools such as factor analysis, t-test and one way analysis of variance and the results are presented in the fourth chapter.

We have also analysed profile, problems, attitude, association between the profile and attitude of employees of these societies and their suggestions for the improvement of the societies. In this part of analysis the statistical tools such as factor analysis, t-test and one way analysis of variance are used.

The book will be very much helpful to the research scholars for carrying out research work in different cooperative sectors, banking industries and in various financial institutions. In general the book will be a good guide to the researchers.

We gratefully thank Dr. A. Meenakshi Sundararajan, the principal of S.T. Hindu College, Nagercoil, the management of S.T.Hindu College, for their constant support and help. We also extend our heartfelt thanks to Dr. S.Chellakumar Rose, Principal of Scott Christian College for his encouragement, support and for being a constant source of inspiration. We express our sincere thanks to our friends and relatives for their help. We also thank Discovery Publishing House Private Ltd., New Delhi for publishing this book.

M. Edwin Gnanadhas

P. Geetha

ACKNOWLEDGEMENTS

We thank the Almighty God who enabled us to complete the work in a successful manner.

We are extremely thankful to the Chairman Secretary, Principal and all the respectable members of the managing committee, S.T. Hindu College, Nagercoil and Scott Christian College for permitting us to pursue the study.

We are immensely grateful to Dr. R. Geetha, Reader in Commerce, V.V. Vaniya Perumal College, Virudhunagar for her critical evaluation and valuable comments that helped us much in improving the quality of the thesis.

We express our sincere thanks to Dr. R. Rathika, Reader in Commerce, Women's Christian College, Nagercoil for her encouragement and valuable suggestion at every stage of our work.

Our sincere thanks to Dr. X. Antony Thanaraj and Dr. M. Jezer Jabanesar, Readers in Commerce, Scott Christian College, Nagercoil and Dr. J.K. Stephen, Principal, Malankara Catholic College, Mariagiri.

Our sincere thanks to Dr. A. Meenakshi Sundara Rajan, Reader in Economics, S.T. Hindu College, Nagercoil and Prof. A. Nagarajan, Dr. N. Sudalayandi Pillai, Prof. V. Kumara Swamy, Dr. T.M. Padmanabhan, Dr. K.V. Soundara Raja, and

Prof. S. Sivasankaran, Department of Commerce of S.T. Hindu College for their encouragement and cooperation for completing my research work.

We are thankful to Mrs. M. Mahalekshmi (S.G.) Lecturer in Commerce, Devi Kumari College, Kuzhithurai for her help and cooperation in completing my research work.

Dr. P. Geetha extremely thankful to her mother, sisters and brothers for their blessings and encouragement to complete the research work.

Our sincere thanks to the staff of cooperative department and secretaries and members of Employees Cooperative Thrift and Credit Societies, who provided me the required data for completing my research work successfully.

We express our heartful thanks to Mr. K. Murugan (husband of Dr. P.Geetha) for his kind cooperation, help and encouragement in each and every stage of the research work.

Our wholehearted thanks to Mrs. Jasmine Janin for the neat typing and kind cooperation for completing my research work.

We also record our deep sense of gratitude to our teachers, colleagues, friends and other well-wishers for their inspiration and support.

M.EDWIN GNANADHAS

P. GEETHA

CONTENTS

1

INTRODUCTION

Co-operative is a way of socio-economic life. The principle of co-operation is as old as the human civilization itself. Mutual help or working together is the essence of co-operative. Co-operative Movement in India is more than 100 years old. It is very sacred and based on the values of self-responsibility, democracy, equality and solidarity. Co-operative members believe in the ethical values of honesty, openness, social responsibility and caring for others.

Cooperation, as a system and thought, plays a vital role in the economic development of the nation. Knowing the importance of Cooperation our leaders such as Jawaharlal Nehru, Mahatma Gandhi and Indira Gandhi paved way for the growth and development of Cooperative Sector in India. Establishment of Cooperatives is regarded as one of the instruments for economic, social and cultural developments as well as human advancement in developing countries.

Planning Commission, Ministry of Finance and Ministry of Commerce have accepted the contribution of cooperative sector in the growth and development of Indian Economy. Nehru said:

> "The idea of Cooperation is something much more than merely an efficient and economic way of doing things. It

is economic, it is fair, it equalises and prevents disparities from growing. But it is something even deeper than that. It is really a way of life."[1]

Cooperation means working together for the achievement of a common goal. It is a method by which individuals with limited resources are enabled to take part in an organised economic activity for mutual benefits through mutual sharing of responsibility for management on the basis of equal partnership.

Dr. K.N. Katja says:

"Co-operation is self-help as well as mutual help. It is a joint enterprise of those who are not financially strong and cannot stand on their own legs and therefore, come together not with a view to get profits but to overcome disability arising out of want of adequate financial resources and thus better their economic conditions."[2]

Indian Co-operative Societies Act, 1912, Section 4(c) considers a co-operative society as "a society which has as its object the promotion of the economic interests of its members in accordance with co-operative principles[3]".

COOPERATIVE BANKING

The co-operative banking structure is pyramidal or federal in character. At the base, that is, at the village level, there is primary credit society upon which the whole edifice of co-operative credit is based.

These societies are federated at the district level into a central society called the Central Co-operative Bank. At the state level, the district banks are federated into an Apex Bank. The Apex or State Co-operative Bank in its turn is closely linked with the National Bank for Agriculture and Rural Development.

Initially, District Central Co-operative Banks and Primary Agricultural Co-operative Societies were financing the short-term credit requirements of the agricultural sector and village artisans for carrying out their endeavours. Parallel to this, land mortgage banks were in existence for meeting long term requirements of the agricultural sector. A subsequent off-shot was the urban co-operative banking movement which came into existence to serve the modest credit requirements of the middle class section of the urban population.

The non-agricultural co-operative credit in India has been growing due to the dedicated initiative of co-operatives and community members without any direct inputs from the government. It has now developed into a self-supporting financial constituency which is today in a position to compete in the de-regulated financial domain, with the banks as well as the non-banking financial institutions as the main players.

The credit societies along with urban co-operative banks constitute the most important and growing segment of the co-operative sector which is totally self-reliant and most vibrant. The Employees' Co-operative Credit Societies are the major non-agricultural credit co-operatives catering to the financial needs of the professional classes of people. They are especially helpful to the salaried class by providing consumption and other loans.

Provision of loans to the members and inculcation of the principle of thrift and savings in the minds of the members are two important functions of these societies. The deposits mobilized are recycled in the same local area, from where the deposits have come.

EMPLOYEES CO-OPERATIVE THRIFT AND CREDIT SOCIETY (ECTCS)

The co-operative movement was started in India to ameliorate the conditions of the rural masses. However, it was soon realised that co-operation offers solution to the difficulties encountered not only by the agriculturalists but also by the urban people in respect of credit as well as other aspects of their business and life. The Maclagan Committee on Co-operation pointed out as early as in 1915 that:

> "Urban credit societies might serve useful purpose in training the upper middle classes to understand ordinary banking principles."

In 1931, the Central Banking Enquiry Committee recommended that:

> "We do not see any objection to special societies for salary-earners if these societies are looked upon as thrift societies for collecting and investing the savings of their members."[4]

Thrift means economy or care in spending of money or using of material. Chambers Universal Learners dictionary defines thrift as:

> "careful spending of money or using of food or other resources so that one can save or have some left in reserve economy."[5]

In the *Encyclopaedia of Social Sciences*, it is said:

> "Although thrift originally connotes saving, the term thrift has a tendency both in technical and in popular discussions to become identified with economic rationality in general with the 'wise' and efficient use and disposal of all resources, time, labour and material things as well as money. The thrifty person is one who resists the temptation to satisfy all monetary whims, but husbands his resources for the satisfaction of one's 'true' needs and desires."[6]

Separate Employees Credit Co-operative Societies have been organised for different categories of workers. Even in the same undertaking there are credit societies for each department or section. At present, there are employees societies:

- exclusively for a single Government department;
- for several Government departments;
- for local board employees;
- for Government as well as local board employees;
- for employees of individual or commercial firms, factories and mills.[7]

Employees Co-operative Thrift and Credit Societies have to be registered as a co-operative society under the Tamil Nadu Cooperative Societies Act. It should have the following objects:

1. to encourage thrift, self-help and co-operation among the members

2. to borrow funds from members and from institutions for being utilised as loans to the members
3. to act as agents for the joint purchase of domestic and other requirements of the members.

MANAGEMENT OF THE ECTCS

The management of the affairs of the society is vested in the hands of Board of Directors. The Board should consists of eleven members of whom at least three should be women and at least two from scheduled castes and scheduled tribes. The members of the Board should be elected by all the members of the society. If the government or the financing Bank has taken share or given financial assistance, it can nominate one person to the Board.

The Board of Directors should meet once in a month and the quorum for the meeting should be four. All questions before the Board should be decided by a majority of votes. Every decision of the Board has to be taken only at an extraordinary meeting convened in accordance with the provisions of the Act.

The President has a overall control over the affairs of society. He has the power to make arrangements for proper maintenance of accounts and custody of cash and other properties of the society. The Secretary should be the officer to sue or to be sued on behalf of the society and bonds in favour of the society should be in the name of the Secretary.

For the past four years, election was not conducted and the societies have been administered by the Special Officers appointed by the Cooperative Department.

Membership

Any person employed permanently can become the member of the Employees Co-operative Thrift and Credit Societies. The application for admission of membership has to be accompanied by agreements in the forms prescribed under the Act. The agreements will be in operation as long as the applicant continues to be the member of the society. He should not be adjudged as insolvent and sentenced for any offence involving moral turpitude.

Application for admission as members and for allotment of shares should be made to the Secretary in the form prescribed by the society. The application has to be disposed off by the Board of Directors. Every member has to subscribe at least one share and the maximum number of shares subscribed by a member should not exceed 2000. He has to pay entrance fee. No member is permitted to withdraw any of the shares within two years from the date, he was admitted as a member. In the event of death of a member the nominee of the deceased will be admitted by the Board of Directors as member of the society. The member's liability continues for two years after the cessation of membership. No member is permitted to transfer his share or create a charge in respect of the same in terms of another member except with the previous sanction of the Board.

Deposits

The Board of Directors may receive deposits from members, associate members and institutions with the approval of the Registrar of Co-operative Societies. The Board can accept two kinds of Deposits namely:

(a) Fixed Deposits

(b) Recurring Deposits.

Fixed deposits are accepted in the multiples of Rs.100 for a period of one year, two years, three years, five years and above. The interest for fixed deposits is calculated at one per cent more than the rate of interest allowed by the financing Bank. The interest on a fixed deposit will cease on the expiry of the period for which the deposit was made unless the notice for renewal of deposit for not less than one year is received from the depositor.

The society offers a recurring deposit scheme under which a fixed amount in the multiples of Rs. 10 has to be deposited for 12, 24, 48 or 60 months. The depositor has to pay monthly deposit before the end of every calendar month.

Maximum borrowing limits are prescribed by the society and they should not exceed ten times the paid up share capital plus the reserve fund.

Loans

Loans on the security of deposit other than thrift deposit are granted to the members. The Board of Directors is the authority to dispose off the loan requisitions.

The applications for loans have to be made to the secretary in the prescribed form and the secretary in turn places them before the Board of Directors. The loans are granted for the following purposes:

(a) Liquidation of debts;

(b) Illness of the member and his dependents;

(c) Marriage, funeral or other ceremonies;

(d) Obligatory religious rites;

(e) Education of children, dependents or relatives of the members;

(f) Purchase of essential items for the families of members;

(g) Any other purpose according to the discretion of Board of Directors.

Any misapplication of the loan will lead to recovery of loan with interest. The maximum limit of loan for a member is Rs. 2 lakh. The Board of Directors may grant a loan not exceeding Rs. 100 for every share held by him or 25 times the total salary per month whichever is less. The monthly recoveries should not exceed 50 per cent of monthly salary.

No member is eligible for a second loan on surety before he/she has not repaid not less than six monthly instalments towards the loan previously taken by him/her.

Repayment of Loans

The principal amount of the loan has to be repaid is not more than 180 instalments and the interest is not more than 60 months. The employee may discharge the whole loan in a single payment.

Any sum paid before due date should first be credited towards the principal and fraction if any, has to be credited towards the interest. In case of default, interest will be charged at 2 per cent more than the normal rate of interest per annum from the date of default to the date of repayment.

If an employee ceases to be in service or dies before repayment, entire outstanding amount will become payable to the society. The property mortgaged to the society is released immediately after the repayment of loan and interest in full.

The Board has the power to recall the loan if the employee is dismissed from service or has resigned from the service. The Board may also exercise the right when the value of the properties mortgaged to the society becomes depreciated.

Surety Relief Fund

A surety relief fund is constituted to offer relief to the subscriber of the fund in the event of the death of the principal borrower to whom he stood surety earlier. The subscription would be Rs. 15 or any amount fixed by the Board of Directors payable every month. The surety relief fund is a separate fund which has to be separately invested and interest has to be added to it every year.

Festival Advance

The Board of Directors of the society may also sanction staff festival advance upto a maximum of two months basic salary or a sum of Rs. 4,000 whichever is less. The advance will be recovered within a period of ten months.

Medical Relief

Payment of medical relief is available to the confirmed employee of the society for some special distress and accidents. It is also available to the family members of the employee. The limit of medical relief ranges from Rs. 500 to Rs. 10,000. The relief is available on the submission of bills for payment. Any misuse of the facilities would lead to recovery of the amounts paid to the employee. The claim should be made within three months from the date of payment of money to the Doctor/Hospital or purchase of medicine. This benefit is available only to those employees who have completed five years of service.

Educational Allowances

Educational allowances to the confirmed employees are available from the Employees' Relief Fund for not more than two children of the employees. Up to plus two, only special fees can be claimed and beyond that, special fees and tuition fees can be claimed. The claims will be admitted to those children who pursue their studies in colleges, professional colleges, polytechnic and co-operative training institutes.

The educational allowance will be given for the academic year and the amount has to be claimed within three months from the date of payment of fees.

Reserve Fund

A reserve fund may be created by a society to meet unforeseen losses. It may be drawn upon with the special sanction of the Registrar to meet unforeseen losses. The fund must be utilised for the items mentioned in clauses (a), (b), (c) and (d) of sub-section (1) of Section 68 of Tamil Nadu Co-operative Societies Act. When the reserve fund of the society exceeds 20 per cent of its working capital, the excess may be utilised in the business of society with the sanction of the Registrar.

Dissolution of the Society

The liquidator is appointed to wind up the affairs of the society. In the dissolution of the society, the reserve fund together with the other funds constituted by the society in accordance with its by-laws should be applied by the liquidator to the discharge of the liabilities in the following order namely:

1. Debts of the society;
2. Paid up share capital; and
3. Dividend on paid up share capital at a rate not exceeding six per cent per annum.

The liquidator may require the society to select a trustee or trustees from among the ex-members and/or others. The trustee has to execute a deed in such form as prescribed by the Registrar from time to time.

Miscellaneous

The society has to prepare annually:

1. Statement showing the receipts and disbursements for the year;
2. Profit and Loss Account;
3. Balance Sheet; and
4. Other statements prescribed by the Registrar.

The society has to prepare a list of its members with their addresses as on the last day of each financial year and furnish a copy to the Registrar.

On any dispute related to the members and the society or between the society and any other registered society, the Registrar may decide the dispute himself, transfer it for disposal to any person who has been vested by the State Government with powers or refer it for arbitrations. An application may be made to the civil court having jurisdiction over the subject matter of the decisions or award requesting that the court may enforce the decisions or award as if it were a decree of the court.

ORIGIN AND DEVELOPMENT OF CREDIT SOCIETIES

Germany is the birth place of Cooperative Credit Movement in the world. Famine, poverty, exploitation and indebtedness were the circumstances, which necessitated the introduction of German credit system. A far-reaching innovation in the field of cooperative credit was initiated by Herr F W. Raiffeisen and Herr Franz Schulze In 1850, the first credit society was founded by Herr Franz Schulze. In 1867 the first co-operative law was implemented and was made applicable to the whole of Germany in1889.[8]

COOPERATIVE SECTOR IN INDIA

Unlike in various European countries co-operative movement was introduced in India as a State policy and owes its inauguration to the enactment of the Co-operative Credit Societies Act, 1904.

But before that some experiments in co-operation had started on local initiative. In 1850, some employees feeling the need for money and to avoid the pinch from the money lenders, determined to start a fund to give persons with fixed incomes a chance to borrow money in times of need at equated rates. The fund, thus started, went on up to 1857. The members contributed a fixed sum periodically. Loans were granted on the mortgage of property. These societies found the membership of the educated employees only. In 1901, there were 200 such societies called "NIDHIS" with a membership of 36000 and a working capital of Rs. 2 crore. These NIDHIS which were found mostly in Uttar Pradesh and Bengal, suggested the possibility of introducing 'Co-operation' in India.[9] The first urban credit society saw the light of the day in 1889 when a mutual aid society was registered at Baroda.[10]

Continuous economic development has meant that the laws meant for cooperatives have also to change in keeping with the changes in time. The Madras Cooperative Societies Act of 1932 was amended in 1961 and again amended in 1983 as Tamil Nadu Cooperative Societies Act, 1983, which came into force from13.4.1988.

The Multi Unit Cooperative Societies Act, 1942 was replaced by the Multi State Cooperative Societies Act 1984. This Act was amended in 2002 and came into force from 19th August, 2002.

COOPERATIVE MOVEMENT IN TAMIL NADU

First cooperative society in India namely, The Triplicane Urban Cooperative Society was established in Madras within a few months after the passage of the Co-operative Credit Societies Act 1904. First cooperative credit society of the country was established at a village called Tirur in Chingleput district, Tamil Nadu.[11]

The Central Cooperative Banks in Tamil Nadu form the backbone of the financing system of the cooperative movement. The societies were at first providing credit to their members with the help of loans obtained from the State Government and deposits raised. These sources soon became unequal to the demand. The idea of organising a bank for financing cooperative societies emanated from the late Sir P. Rajagopalachariar, the first Registrar of Cooperative Societies.[12]

The Madras Central Urban Bank was the first bank in Tamil Nadu registered on 19th October, 1905 under Act X of 1904, with the sole object of finding money to finance societies in all parts of the State. With the formation of large number of new societies in the districts, the need was felt for more financing banks and central banks were formed one after another at each district head quarters.

EMPLOYEES CO-OPERATIVE THRIFT AND CREDIT SOCIETIES (ECTCS) IN TAMIL NADU

The number of ECTCS in Tamil Nadu and the members in them for the period from 1996-67 to 2003-04 were collected from various records of Registrar office, Tamil Nadu Co-operative Credit Societies at Chennai. The amount of capital invested in the societies and the reserves in these societies from 1996-97 to 2003-04 are shown in Table 1.1.

Table 1.1

Number of Employees Co-operative Thrift and Credit Societies (E.C.T.C.S) in Tamil Nadu

Year	*Number of Societies*	*Members in Crore*	*Capital (Rs. in Crore)*		
			Working Capital	*Paid up Capital*	*Reserves*
1996-97	1793	102.75	107.93	238.92	72.93
1997-98	1859	144.94	120.75	270.56	72.85
1998-99	1826	118.15	120.44	281.83	74.18
1999-00	1864	118.06	117.75	291.34	69.23
2000-01	1907	117.81	112.97	300.07	68.18
2001-02	1915	118.26	113.33	301.67	68.62
2002-03	1918	126.27	121.91	323.21	71.16
2003-04	1888	126.81	129.87	329.97	78.98

Source: Records of Registrar Office, Tamil Nadu Co-operative Credit Societies, Chennai.

The number of societies in ECTCS was increasing from 1793 in 1996-97 to 1888 in 2003-04. The members in ECTCS were increasing from 102.75 crore to 126.81 crore during the same period. The rate of increase in the members in ECTCS was very low in 2003-04. The working capital in ECTCS was increasing from Rs. 107.83 crore in 1996-97 to Rs. 129.87 crore in 2003-04. The paid up capital was increasing from Rs. 238.92 crore to Rs. 329.97 crore during the same period. The reserves in ECTCS was increasing from Rs. 72.93 crore in 1996-97 to Rs. 78.98 crore in 2003-04.

Loan Disbursement in ECTCS

The medium term and short term loans disbursed by the ECTCS of Tamil Nadu from 1996-97 to 2003-04 are shown in Table 1.2.

Table 1.2

Loan Disbursement by ECTCS of Tamil Nadu

(Rs. in Crore)

Year	*Nature of Loans*		*Total*
	Medium Term	*Short Term*	
1996-97	995.40	50.75	1046.15
1997-98	1098.92	50.46	1149.38
1998-99	1194.96	43.14	1238.10
1999-00	1178.76	55.59	1234.35
2000-01	1161.08	58.93	1220.01
2001-02	1171.13	59.45	1230.58
2002-03	2466.19	12.53	2478.72
2003-04	2582.99	18.95	2601.94

Source: Registrar Office, Tamil Nadu Co-operative Credit Societies.

The medium-term loan disbursed by ECTCS was increasing from Rs. 995.40 crore in 1996-97 to Rs. 2582.99 crore in 2003-04. The rate of increase in the disbursement of medium term loan by the societies during the period of the study was 159.49 per cent. During the same period, the short term loan disbursed was decreasing from Rs. 50.75 crore in 1996-97 to Rs. 18.95 crore in 2003-04. The rate of decrease in the short term loan disbursed during the period of the study was 62.66 per cent. The contribution of medium term loan disbursed to the total loans disbursed in 2003-04 was 99.87 per cent. It reveals the importance of medium term loan disbursement in the loan disbursement among the societies.

Financial Performance of ECTCS in Tamil Nadu

The financial performance of the ECTCS has been analysed with the help of profit they have achieved so far. The number of profit making societies and the total profit achieved by these societies are presented in Table 1.3.

Table 1.3

Financial Performance of ECTCS in Tamil Nadu

Year	*Profit Making*		*Loss Incurring*	
	Number of Societies	*Amount in Crore*	*Number of Societies*	*Amount in Crore*
1996-97	1559	48.39	234	3.49
1997-98	1618	59.00	241	2.91
1998-99	1612	73.67	214	2.94
1999-00	1650	82.28	214	4.58
2000-01	1697	81.46	210	5.55
2001-02	1722	82.68	193	5.67
2002-03	1714	91.35	204	6.53
2003-04	1675	87.98	213	7.03

Source: Records of Registrar Office, Tamil Nadu Co-operative Credit Societies.

The number of profit-making societies constituted 86.95 per cent to the total societies in 1996-97. That percentage of profit making societies increased to 88.72 per cent in 2003-04. The amount of profit achieved by the societies was increasing from Rs.48.39 crore in 1996-97 to Rs.87.98 crore in 2003-04. The rate of increase in profit during the period of the study was 81.44 per cent. The average profit earned by the society in Tamil Nadu in 1996-97 was Rs.0.03 crore whereas in 2003-04, it was 0.05 crore. The loss making societies were decreasing from 234 in 1996-97 to 213 in 2003-04. The total loss in the societies was increasing from Rs. 3.49 crore in 1996-97 to Rs. 7.03 crore in 2003-04. The average loss incurred by the society was increasing from Rs. 0.0149 crore in 1996-97 to Rs. 0.033 crore in 2003-04.

EMPLOYEES CO-OPERATIVE THRIFT AND CREDIT SOCIETIES IN KANYAKUMARI DISTRICT

The ECTCS in Kanyakumari District are classified under two functionaries. One is under the Deputy Registrar of Co-operative Societies at Nagercoil and another is under the Deputy Registrar of Co-operative Societies at Thuckalay. The number of ECTCS and the membership in that societies are given below.

Table 1.4

Number of Societies and Membership in Employees Co-operative Thrift and Credit Societies at Kanyakumari District

Sl. No.	*Name of the Office*	*Number of Societies*	*Number of Membership*
1.	Dy. Registrar office at Nagercoil	26	16,327
2.	Dy. Registrar office at Thuckalay	15	13,203
	Total	41	29,530

Source: Office of the Deputy Registrar, Co-operative Societies at Nagercoil and Thuckalay.

Totally there are 26 ECTCS at Nagercoil whereas only 15 are at Thuckalay and the number of members of the societies are 16,327 and 13,203 respectively.

Performance of the Employees Co-operative Thrift and Credit Societies in Nagercoil

Auditors evaluate the financial performance of the ECTCS and classify them into A, B, C and other grades on the basis of their performances. The performance of A grade societies is better than that of others whereas the C and other grades indicate the poor performance of the societies. The financial performances of the societies were evaluated from 1994-95 to 2003-04. The distribution of societies on the basis of their grades is shown in Table 1.5.

Table 1.5

Different Grades of ECTCS at Nagercoil

Year	*Number of Societies*				*Total*
	'A' grade	*'B' grade*	*'C' grade*	*Others*	
1994-95	6	15	2	0	23
1995-96	9	12	2	0	23
1996-97	7	14	2	0	23
1997-98	7	14	2	0	23
1998-99	8	13	2	0	23
1999-00	7	12	2	1	23
2000-01	9	11	2	1	23
2001-02	11	8	3	1	23
2002-03	7	13	2	1	23
2003-04	8	12	2	1	23

Source: Audit Reports of ECTCS at Nagercoil.

The 'A' grade societies were increased from 6 in 1994-95 to 11 in 2001-02 and then declined to 8 societies in 2003-04. 'B' grade societies were declined from 15 in 1994-95 to 12 societies in 2003-04. The 'C' grade societies were increased from 2 in 1994-95 to 3 in 2001-02 and then declined to 2 societies in 2003-04. It reveals the moderate performance of the societies at Nagercoil.

Performance of the Employees Co-operative Thrift and Credit Societies in Thuckalay

The financial performances of the societies were evaluated from 1994-95 to 2003-04. The distribution of societies on the basis of their grades is shown in Table 1.6.

Table 1.6

Different Grades of ECTCS at Thuckalay

Year	*Number of Societies*				*Total*
	'A' grade	*'B' grade*	*'C' grade*	*Others*	
1994-95	3	2	6	2	13
1995-96	3	3	4	3	13
1996-97	3	3	4	3	13
1997-98	3	3	5	2	13
1998-99	5	2	3	3	13
1999-00	4	3	5	1	13
2000-01	3	5	5	0	13
2001-02	3	4	4	2	13
2002-03	3	3	6	1	13
2003-04	2	4	5	2	13

Source: Audit Reports of ECTCS at Thuckalay.

The number of 'A' grade societies was decreased from 3 in 1994-95 to 2 in 2003-04 whereas the number of 'B' grade societies was increased from 2 to 4 during the same period. At the same time, the number of 'C' grade societies was ranging from 3 to 6 societies. The number of other group of societies was ranging from 3 to 0 during the period of study.

STATEMENT OF THE PROBLEM

The Employees Co-operative Credit Societies have been very badly affected by the adoption of new economic policy of the Government of India in 1991. Due to voluntary retirement scheme and dwindling number of office employees, salary earners sector has been adversely affected. The membership strength of such societies has been decreasing due to policies such as VRS schemes and curtailment of number of posts. The capital base of these societies has been eroded. The persons who are forced to leave the co-operative societies due to such policies suffer psychologically as well as economically. The personnel working in the societies do not prefer to continue for more number of years due to inadequate salary in commensurate with their educational qualifications. The employees working in the ECTCS are not well paid. The ECTCS are subjected to so many problems like duel control, untrained human capital, limited area of operation, lack of marketing view, limited resources, lack of proper support from the Government, problem of recovery, lack of computerization, lack of transparency and incomplete corporate governance.

In the competitive environment, the survival and future of the ECTCS depend upon their performances. Survival of the societies depend upon their capability to provide the services to the customers. Needless to emphasise that the capacity of the societies to provide better services depends upon their employees. The service giving capacity of societies can be directly linked to the efficiency and effectiveness of the employees. It also depends upon the members' attitude towards the services offered by the societies. The attitudes of the members and the employees are inevitable for the successful performance of these societies. But the attitudes of these two sections are not favourable to the societies because of so many problems in the societies. They are the major hurdles for the performance and progress of the ECTCS.

NEED FOR THE STUDY

The winds of economic liberalisation and globalisation have been sweeping our economy for nearly a decade. But the sector of the economy, which has remained untouched by this wind, is the co-operative sector. This is particularly worrying since co-operatives play an important role in the economy of a number of States. The non-agricultural co-operative credit in India has been growing due to the dedicated initiative of co-operatives and community members without any direct inputs from the government. It has now developed into a self-supporting financial constituency which is today in a position to compete in the de-regulated financial domain, with the banks as well as non-banking financial institutions as the main players.

The credit societies along with urban co-operative banks constitute the most important and growing segment of the co-operative sector which is totally self reliant and most vibrant. Operations of credit co-operative societies in urban areas, are less complicated than those of full-fledged banks and they cater to the requirements of limited group of individuals who are their members. Among these societies a sizeable and potential portion is that of salary earners' societies. A very large number of co-operative organisations in public as well as private sector and government offices where a sizeable number of employees work, generally have their own credit societies, which are managed by the members of staff.

The co-operative societies especially ECTCS have been facing a series of problems of fall in membership, poor performance, high labour turnover and poor service quality. The changes in Government policies and the downswing of employment and the constraints imposed by the existing laws affect the societies to a greater extent. On one side, the members of the societies are declining because of Voluntary Retirement Schemes and also the State Government's ban on the new recruitment. On another side, the foreign and private banks are competing with the public and co-operative banks in the provision of service quality to their customers.

OBJECTIVES OF THE STUDY

The objectives of the study are:

1. To appraise the working of the Employees Co-operative Thrift and Credit Societies in Kanyakumari District.
2. To study the profile of the members of the societies.
3. To reveal the members' attitude towards the society and the problems encountered by the members.

4. To analyse the association between the profile of the members and their attitude towards the society;
5. To exhibit the profile of the employees working in the societies;
6. To identify the employees' attitude towards the society and the problems encountered by them;
7. To examine the relationship between the profile of the employees and their attitude towards the society;
8. To reveal the employees' view on the measures to improve the functioning of the societies; and
9. To offer suggestions based on the findings of the study.

RESEARCH METHODOLOGY

Research methodology is the way of systematically solving the research problem. It enlightens the methods to be followed in research activities starting from investigation to presentation. It includes, research design, locale of research, sample and sampling framework, methods of data collection, framework of analysis and limitations.

Research Design of the Study

A research design is a framework or blueprint for conducting the research project. It details the procedures necessary for obtaining the information needed to structure and/ or solve research problems.

For this study, the researcher has used the already available facts or information and analysed them to make a critical evaluation of the performance of the co-operative thrift societies. The survey and fact-finding enquiries were conducted to identify the prospects and problems of the societies among the members and employees of the societies. So the present study is descriptive and analytical in nature.

Locale of Research

While studying the co-operative thrift societies, it was imperative to select the members and employees of the ECTCS

Hence, it was decided to select the registered ECTCS in Kanyakumari District. Since the District has two revenue divisions namely Nagercoil and Thuckalay, the societies were selected from the two revenue divisions through a specified sampling framework.

Selection of the Study Area

Kanyakumari was purposively selected as the study area by the researcher for the following reasons:

1. There were no recent exclusive studies about the problems and prospects of the ECTCS, in Kanyakumari District.
2. The researcher is one of the members of the ECTCS, at Nagercoil.
3. Familiarity to culture, local dialect and infrastructural facilities available would help the researcher to develop a good rapport with the societies' members and employees. Hence, better and valid responses could be received.

Description of Study Area

Kanyakumari District is surrounded by majestic hills and plains bordered by colourful sea-shores, fringed with coconut trees and paddy fields, here and there are a few elevated patches of red cliffs with undulating valleys and plains between the mountainous terrain and the sea-coast, so closely interwoven with Temples and Churches and other edifices. With an area of 1672 sq.km, it occupies 1.29 per cent of the total extent of Tamil Nadu. It ranks first in literacy among the districts in Tamil Nadu.

Kanyakumari is the southern most district of Tamil Nadu. The district lies between 77°15′ and 77°36′ of the eastern longitudes and 8°03′ and 8°35′ of the northern latitudes. The District is bound by Tirunelveli District on the north and the east. The south eastern boundary is the Gulf of Mannar. On the south and the south-west the boundaries are the Indian Ocean and the Arabian Sea. On the west and the north-west it is bound by Kerala.

Demographic Profile of the District

The people are the human resource of the district. Their culture, religion, aptitude, habits, beliefs, talents etc. have a bearing on how the district presents itself to others. Tamil and Malayalam are the main languages of this district. Hindus and Christians form a sizeable percentage of the population of the district and there are a number of Muslims dominated belts in this district.

Kanyakumari District consists of 13 blocks. The areas in Thovalai and Agasteeswaram blocks are 360.91 and 143.35 sq.km. The higher population is identified in Nagercoil Municipality and Munchirai with the population of 1,90,084 and 1,75,454 respectively. The higher literate population are identified in Nagercoil Municipality and Melapuram with the literate population of 1,52,274 and 1,20,296 respectively.[13] The literacy rate is noticed as an average of 76.0 per cent in the district.

Revenue Administration

Kanyakumari District consists of two Revenue Divisions namely Nagercoil and Padmanabhapuram, each headed by a Revenue Officer. The Nagercoil Revenue Division consists of two Taluks: Agasteeswaram with its headquarters at Nagercoil and Thovalai with its headquarters at Boothapandi. The Padmanabhapuram Revenue Division consists of two Taluks: Kalkulam with its headquarters at Thuckalay and Vilavancode with its headquarters at Kuzhithurai. These Taluks are administered by Tahsildars.

Sources of Data

The study is based on both primary and secondary data.

Primary data with regard to the profile of the members and the employees, their attitude towards the society and the problems encountered by the members and employees of the societies were collected from the members and employees of the ECTCS with the help of structured schedules designed and finalised after a pilot survey.

Secondary data such as number of members, share capital, thrift deposit, profit, reserves, incomes, investments, expenditures and all other financial data were collected from audit reports and records of the respective ECTCS at Nagercoil and at Thuckalay and from the records of Deputy Registrar's Office at Nagercoil and Thuckalay. State level data were collected from the records of the Office of the Registrar of Co-operative Societies, Chennai.

Sampling Procedure

The total number of ECTCS in Nagercoil and Thuckalay revenue divisions are 26 and 15 respectively. Out of these societies, only 23 and 13 societies are keeping their accounting information for the recent past 10 years. So only the societies which are keeping accounting facts are purposively selected for the study. The above said 23 and 13 societies have 15,499 and 12,771 members respectively. The total sample size of members has arbitrarily assigned as two per cent of the total population. So the sample size is 564 members. Proportionate stratified sampling method is followed for selecting the sample members. The distribution of members and sample members in the present study is shown in Table 1.7.

Table 1.7

Distribution of Members and Sample Members Selected for the Study

Total Members		*Sample Members*	
Societies at Nagercoil	*Societies at Thuckalay*	*Societies at Nagercoil*	*Societies at Thuckalay*
1	*2*	*3*	*4*
310	461	6	9
5046	1654	101	33
85	1570	2	31
440	2402	8	48
77	415	2	8

(Contd...)

1	2	3	4
528	885	11	18
226	1468	5	29
96	1517	2	30
947	1102	19	22
249	201	5	4
1278	301	26	6
303	384	6	8
599	411	12	8
1683		34	
444		9	
257		5	
931		18	
184		3	
871		17	
255		5	
270		5	
240		5	
180		4	
15499	12771	310	254

Source: Audit reports of the societies.

In order to study the employees' perception on the societies, from each society two employees have been selected at random. The total employees selected for the study are 72.

Tools Used for Analysis

For analysing the data collected during investigation, the following statistical tools were used. They are based upon the nature of data and relevance of the information required.

T-test

The parameters from two different populations are tested with the help of 't' test. The 't' statistics is calculated by

$$t = \frac{\overline{X}_1 - \overline{X}_2}{\sqrt{\frac{(n_1 - 1)\sigma_{s1}^{\;2} + (n_2 - 1)\sigma_{s2}^{\;2}}{n_1 + n_2 - 2}} \times \sqrt{\frac{1}{n_1} + \frac{1}{n_2}}}$$

with the degree of freedom of $(n_1 + n_2 - 2)$

whereas t = t-statistics

$\overline{X}_1$ = Mean of the first sample

$\overline{X}_2$ = Mean of the second sample

σ_{S1}^2 = Variance in the first sample

σ_{S2}^2 = Variance in the second sample

n_1 = Number of samples in the first group

n_2 = Number of samples in the second group

Analysis of Variance

Analysis of Variance was used for examining the differences in the mean values of the dependent variables associated with the effect of controlled independent variables, after taking into account the influence of the uncontrolled independent variables. Essentially, ANOVA is used as a test of means of two or more populations. One way analysis of variance involves only one categorical variable or a single factor ANOVA applied when that categorical variable is in interval scale.

$$F\ ratio = \frac{Variance\ between\ groups}{Variance\ within\ groups}$$ is calculated and compared

with the respective table value of F, [(k-1)/(n-k+1)] degree of freedom whereas k-number of groups, n-number of samples.

Multiple Regression Analysis

Multiple regression analysis is used when there is one dependent variable and more than one independent variables. Both these independent and dependent variables are in interval scale. The impact of independent variables on the dependent variable is measured with the help of multiple regression. The fitted regression model was

$$y = a+b_1x_1+b_2x_2+ \ldots\ldots\ldots +b_nx_n+e$$

where y = Dependent variable

$x_1 \ldots\ldots\ldots x_n$ = Independent variables

$b_1 \ldots b_n \ldots$ = Regression coefficient of independent variables

a = intercept and

e = error term.

Factor Analysis

Factor analysis is a general name denoting a class of procedures primarily used for data reduction and summarization. In research, there may be a large number of variables, most of which are correlated and which must be reduced to a manageable level. Relationships among sets of many interrelated variables were examined and represented in terms of underlying factors.

Growth Rate Analysis

The statistical figures relating to various financial facts of E.C.T.C.S were compiled and analysed by fitting trend equation.

The equation is $y = a+bx$

Whereas y = financial fact

x = time

a = Intercept and

b = coefficient

Compound growth rates of these variables are estimated to ascertain the growth performance in the societies. The type of function fitted is in the form of

$y = ab^t$

where

y = Value of financial facts.

a = intercept

b = parameter

t = years

By taking logarithms of above equation on both sides, the exponential form gets reduced to linear form with (yt) as dependent variable and 't' as independent variable. The transformation is given as follows:

In Yt = In A + In B

The equation is solved by ordinary least squares method. The parameters 'a' and 'b' will indicate absolute investment in various financial facts. In order to obtain compound growth rate it is necessary to take antilog of 'b' and subtract one from it. The so obtained value is multiplied by 100 to get percentage growth rate.

Compound growth rate = (Antilog of b-1) × 100

SCOPE OF THE STUDY

The study also throw light on the members' perception and employees' perception on the various functions of the societies. The analysis would also reveal the association between the profiles of the members, and the employees and their perception on the various functions of the societies. The present study is confined only to Kanyakumari district. The period of the study covers ten years from 1994-95 to 2003-2004. The study limits its scope on the functioning of the societies which have full financial facts during the above said study period. The interviews among the members and employees were conducted during the year 2005-06. The results of the study would be useful to the societies and policy makers to formulate appropriate policies to augment the efficient working of the societies.

LIMITATIONS OF THE STUDY

A few Employees Cooperative Thrift and Credit Societies of Kanyakumari district are not included for the study because of the non-availability of the complete records for the whole study period.

The financial facts are collected only from the audit reports of the individual societies. The audit reports of the societies are available only up to the period of 2003-04. So the study covers only a period of ten years from 1994-95 to 2003-04.

CHAPTER SCHEME

For lucid presentation, the present study has been classified into six chapters:

Chapter One includes the introduction, the Employees Co-operative Thrift and Credit Societies in Tamil Nadu and in Kanyakumari District, statement of the problem, objectives and research methodology of the study.

Chapter Two narrates the various concepts used in the present study and the review of literature of the previous studies.

Chapter Three examines the financial performance of Employees Co-operative Thrift and Credit Societies in Kanyakumari District.

Chapter Four consists of the profile of the members, their attitude towards the societies, problems encountered by them and the measures for the improvement of the societies.

Chapter Five reveals the attitude of the employees of the societies, problems encountered by them and the important measures to improve the service facilities.

Chapter Six includes the summary of findings, suggestions and conclusion.

REFERENCES

1. Dwivedi R.C., *Jawaharlal Nehru: His Vision of Cooperative*, New Delhi, 1989, p. 9.

2. Bedi R.D., *Theory, History and Practice of Co-operation*, New Delhi, 1966, p. 15.

3. Mathur B.S, *Cooperation in India*, Sahitya Bhawan, Agra, 1992, p. 9.

4. *Report of the Central Banking Committee*, 1931, Vol. 1, Part 1, p. 255.

5. *The Chambers Universal Dictionary*, International Students Edition, Macmillan India Ltd., Delhi, 1983, p. 789.

6. *Encyclopeadia of the Social Sciences*, Macmillian India Ltd., New Delhi, 1954, p. 623.

7. The Tamil Nadu Cooperative Manual 1965, Government of Tamil Nadu, 1972. p. 58.

8. Bedi, R.D.,*op.cit.*, p. 106.

9. *Ibid.*, p. 11.

10. Mathur, B.S., *op.cit.*, p. 221.

11. Thirunarayanan, R., *Cooperative Banking in India*, New Delhi, 1996, p. 20.

12. *Ibid.*, p. 31.

13. *District Profile*, (2005), Collectorate, Nagercoil.

2

CONCEPTS AND REVIEW OF LITERATURE

CONCEPTS

The financial performance of the ECTCS has been measured with the help of ratio analysis. The important ratios calculated in the present study are discussed in this chapter.

The societies' financial performance has been analysed with the help of operational efficiency, financial efficiency and liquidity efficiency.

Operational Ratios

The operational efficiency refers to the most efficient use of resources, so as to generate optimum returns. Modern banking activities are becoming complex, necessitating broader knowledge and a proper information system to improve financial performance. The operational efficiency of the societies has been measured with the help of the following ratios.

(a) ***Own funds to borrowed funds ratio*****:**

$$\text{Own funds to borrowed funds} = \frac{\text{Own funds}}{\text{Borrowed funds}} \times 100$$

Own funds include share capital, statutory reserves and balance of profit and loss account and borrowed funds include the deposits and borrowings of the bank.

(b) *Borrowings to working capital ratio*:

This ratio indicates the proportion of borrowings to working capital and is worked out by the formula

$$\frac{\text{Borrowing}}{\text{Working Capital}} \times 100$$

In the present study, borrowings refer to borrowings from other banks and financial institutions and working capital includes share capital, reserves, deposits and borrowings less investments in fixed assets (land and premises, furniture and fittings, etc.).

(c) *Credit to deposit ratio*:

This ratio is calculated by the formula:

$$\frac{\text{Credit}}{\text{Deposit}} \times 100$$

Credit includes all types of loans and advances disbursed during the year and deposit includes all deposits collected by the bank during the respective year. A higher ratio implies the efficiency in deploying the funds profitably. This ratio is mainly used to know the total credit of the bank as a percentage of the total deposits. It represents the bank's efficiency with regard to the turnover of funds which the societies have raised other than share capital.

(d) *Outstanding loans to working capital ratio*:

This ratio measures the credit granting capacity of the societies. This ratio is calculated by the formula:

$$\frac{\text{Outstanding Loan}}{\text{Working Capital}} \times 100$$

Profitability Ratios

The financial efficiency of the societies has been examined with the help of the profitability ratios of the societies. These ratios are:

(i) Total expenses to total income;

(ii) Net profit to working capital;

(iii) Interest paid to interest received; and

(iv) Non-interest expenses to non-interest income.

The ratio of total expenses to total income is calculated by

$$\frac{\text{Total Expenditure}}{\text{Total Income}} \times 100$$

The total expenditure includes all operating and non-operating expenses incurred by the societies and total income includes all income received by the societies from operating and non-operating nature. For a society to become profitable total expenditure must be less than the total income.

The net profit to working capital ratio represents the bank's efficiency in making higher returns out of the working capital. The net profit should be adequate enough to provide optimum returns on the working capital. This ratio is calculated by the formula:

$$\frac{\text{Net Profit}}{\text{Working Capital}} \times 100$$

The higher ratio indicates more profitability of the societies.

The interest paid is the amount paid on deposits and borrowings whereas interest received is the amount received by the bank on loans and advances and investments. Interest paid and profitability have an inverse relationship. This is not applicable in the case of interest received. It has a direct relationship with profitability. As the interest received increases profitability also increases. This ratio has been worked out by the formula:

$$\frac{\text{Interest paid}}{\text{Interest received}} \times 100$$

The non-interest expense to non-interest income ratio is worked out to find out the bank's expenses and income other than the interest paid and received. The formula used for this ratio is

$$\frac{\text{Non-interest Expenses}}{\text{Non-interest Income}} \times 100$$

Liquidity Ratios

Societies raise funds mainly by mobilising deposits. Funds raised in the form of deposits are to be profitably employed for the effective functioning of a society. But at the time of employing funds, they have to consider the liquidity also. But for the sake of liquidity it is not advisable to keep large proportions of the deposits as idle cash which does not generate any income. Therefore, a proper balance should be struck between liquidity and profitability. The liquidity efficiency of the societies is analysed with the help of three ratios:

(i) Cash in hand and at bank to borrowed funds;

(ii) Investment to deposits; and

(iii) Spread to total assets.

Cash is kept with the society to meet the demands of the depositors. Higher the cash maintained in the banks higher will be the liquidity and *vice-versa*. And higher the cash maintained in the bank less will be the profitability and vice-versa. The following formula is used for calculating the ratio:

$$\frac{\text{Cash in Hand and at Bank}}{\text{Borrowed Funds}} \times 100$$

In the present study, the cash in hand and at bank represent balances in hand, balances with other banks and money at call and short notice.

Investment to deposits indicates the relationship between investment made by the societies and the deposits received for the societies. It is used to study the extent to which deposits are invested by the societies. The higher ratio indicates the higher portion of deposits invested in some form. The formula used to study the relationship is

$$\frac{\text{Investment}}{\text{Deposits}} \times 100$$

The spread to total assets ratio represents the contribution of spread in total assets of the society. The spread is the difference between interest received and interest paid in the society. The ratio of spread to total assets indicates the contribution of operating income in the total assets. It is calculated by

$$\frac{\text{Spread}}{\text{Total Assets}} \times 100$$

The higher ratio indicates the higher contribution of spread in total assets.

REVIEW OF LITERATURE

It is relevant to review briefly the previous studies made in the related areas of the present study. The reviews related to the present study are classified under four headings namely, performance of Co-operative Societies, viability of Co-operative Societies, attitude of members and employees of Co-operative Societies and problems and prospects of Co-operative Societies.

Performance of Co-operative Societies

Suhag *et al.* (1998)[1] found that the number of borrowers in Primary Land Development Banks was high in the category of small and marginal farmers. Flow and stock of loans too were higher in small and marginal farmers category. The highest delinquency rate was about 96 per cent in 1986-87 whereas the same was higher in category of small and marginal farmers as 87 per cent. The management cost and transaction costs were quite higher in PLDBs.

Narasimha Reddy *et al.* (1998)[2] have used fifteen different financial ratios to evaluate the performance of the four selected silk handloom weavers' co-operative societies. The solvency ratios indicated that these societies had creditors for the transactions. The dues paid by the societies with high rate of interests reduced their profit share. The liquidity ratios were slow unity. There was a stabilisation in total earnings of these societies over years. The sales turnover ratios were found to be positive.

Asthana and Manali (1999)[3] observed that the important strength of urban co-operative banks is low cost of raising deposits and giving loans, high contacts in market, disciplinary control of directors, low competition and less liabilities whereas the weaknesses are certain limitations being a co-operative bank from RBI, lobbying, low customer orientation, negligible marketing especially in the area of marketing and limited area of operation.

Devaraja (1999)[4] revealed that the credit gap between Primary Agricultural Societies and Hassan District Central Co-operative Bank is widening from year to year. The main cause of that credit gap is the co-operative dues and the writing-off interest dues from the farmers. The increase in overdue position of the bank is caused by its poor recovery performance of the bank. The important cause for overdue among the borrowers is the diversification of credit from agriculture to non-agricultural purposes.

Devaraja (1999)[5] revealed that the cooperative society concentrating on the production of honey and bee-wax has a good turnover and profits. The society has to make itself very strong, attractive and efficient in its behavioural and operational attitude, only then it can stand and operate in the market. The capital structure of the societies is very sound.

Padmini and Jaish (1999)[6] examined the financial performance of Regional Rural Banks with the help of important ratios namely owned funds to borrowed funds, borrowings to working capital, credit deposits ratio, outstanding loans to working capital, total expenditure to total income, net profit to working capital, interest paid to interest received, non-interest expense to non-interest income and cash in hand and at bank to borrowed funds.

Subbiah (1999)[7] concluded that the financial soundness of any lending institution largely depends upon its success in the recovery of loans. Good recovery of loans helps for the proper recycling of funds and poor recovery results in the depletion of resources. The study revealed the highest growth rate in outstanding credit. The recovery performance declined from 70 per cent to 66 per cent during the study period.

Deepak and Agarwal (1999)[8] found that the most costly source of borrowing in Dairy societies is a loan from District Central Co-operative Bank. This source is also not a reliable one. The main source of borrowing for all the societies is from Government schemes which is relatively cheaper. The profitability is highly affected by the higher cost of funds borrowed from the District Central Co-operative Banks.

Yadav (1999)[9] analysed the performance and prospects of agricultural cooperative credit societies in Uttar Pradesh. The compound growth rate of reserve fund of the bank is greater than the compound growth rate of share capital. The share capital and reserve fund constituted own fund and its compound growth rate at the state level and national level are 11.05 and 11.76 per cent respectively. The DCBs in Kerala could not advance loans equal to the national growth rate. The compound growth rate of loans overdue at the state and national levels are 12.12 per cent and 10.60 per cent respectively.

Dash (2000)[10] examined the financial performance of cooperative bank in Jamnagar, Gujarat through ratio analysis. He evaluated the financial performance through operational ratios, profitability ratios, productivity ratios and solvency ratios. He concluded that, despite satisfactory financial performance in the bank, there are certain grey areas which need immediate attention. These are capital base, professionals, diversification of loans, innovative activities and increase in service quality.

Padmini (2000)[11] found the maximum compound growth rate of deposits in Ernakulam bank whereas the minimum was noticed in Palakad bank. In loans and advances, the maximum and minimum compound growth rates were seen in Ernakulam and Idukki banks. In the case of fixed assets, and investment also, the maximum and minimum compound growth rates were identified in the Ernakulam and Idukki banks. The study also revealed that the majority of the parameters showed a constant and proportional increase over time.

Singh and Kaur (2000)[12] analysed the performance of agricultural cooperative service societies in Punjab. They found that supply of untimely and substandard inputs by federal/ government agencies hampered the performance of primary societies. Further, populistic government policies, factionalism and insecurity of employees of the societies too contributed to the failure of these societies. The identified important attributes of success/failure of cooperative societies are efficient management and cooperation/interest of villages.

Teli (2006)[13] assessed the progress of different indicators of urban co-operative banks in Kolhapur District. It was indicated by a considerable growth in their membership, share capital, reserves, owned funds, deposits, loans and net profits. But at the same time increase in overdues and number of banks making losses reflected an urgent need for further investigation of the working of the VCBs in that district.

Rao *et al.* (2000)[14] found that the compound growth rate of financial indicators of Kavinagar District Cooperative Central Bank namely total share capital, paid-up share capital, deposits utilized, investments, total liabilities, current assets, current liabilities, income, expenditure and advances outstanding were found to be statistically significant. Authorised share capital, credit disbursed, recovery percentage were statistically not significant.

Masthan and Narayanasamy (2000)[15] measured the growth in membership, share capital, deposits, working capital, loans and advances, investment, cost of management etc., in Chittoor Co-operative town bank. The yearly increase in membership reveals the continuation of faith by the members. The high growth of share capital is also in line with the high growth of membership during the same period. There is a positive growth in deposits year after year. The growth of reserves is very high during the study period and this indicates the substantial allocation from profits towards reserves such as building funds, reserve fund, employee welfare funds and NPA provisions.

Lopoyetum (2000)[16] revealed a reasonable performance in deposit mobilization and credit deployment. However, the extent of overdues was found increasing in absolute terms over a period of time though the bank was exerting much pressure on recovery operation. The non-performing advances poses a significant threat to the rural institutions, whereas the effectiveness and efficiency of credit management largely hinges on prompt repayment of loans/advances. The overall recovery status of the rural financing banks is therefore far from satisfactory.

Kumar (2001)[17] revealed that the banks' performance in mobilization of deposits was good during the study period. The credit-deposit ratio came down during this period. It indicates that the bank could not utilize these deposits to the maximum extend for giving loans and advances. So the bank keeps more surplus funds. The analysis of recovery performance of the bank also showed that it was not so satisfactory. It is also one of the reasons for low profit of the bank.

Rengasamy (2001)[18] observed that interest rate spread, salary and other expenses of the Cooperative Urban Bank jointly account for 87 per cent of variations in its net profit. The coefficient of interest spread is positively related to the net profit. The variable salary and other expenses are found to have a negative effect on the net profits.

Ali and Banahar (2001)[19] identified that the co-operative oil mills achieved break even quantity of production. The margin of safety in value of products to be produced was negative in case of large scale unit on one hand and huge capacity was unutilised on the other hand. The liquidity ratios were less than the standard ratios during the study period. The average value of net profits to funds ratio was also very low. The inventory ratio was identified as lesser in large scale mills compared to the medium scale mills.

Sahayoga (2002)[20] found that the human resource development is one of the drawbacks of the urban cooperative banks. Lack of scientific method of selection, lack of knowledge and skill required for their jobs and lack of support from the management led to their low performance.

Raihar (2002)[21] in his study on growth, profitability and cost efficiency of urban co-operative banks in India revealed that the growth of profits is negative in the banks whereas the growth of advances are positive. The cost efficiency in the urban co-operative banks is not at an appreciable level. The higher expense ratios are identified with the respective income ratios.

Zahir Hussain (2003)[22] found that there has been a spectacular increase in the membership, deposits raised and loans granted by the bank. The recovery is around 90 per cent. The management of the bank is responsible to the changing economic environment and customer requirements. The bank has established its creditability in the district.

Dayanandan and Sasikumar (2003)[23] used the chain based index to measure the growth of deposits, owned funds, borrowings, total assets, income and expenditure of the co-operative banks at Kerala. The results showed that the deposits were declining because of unattractive rate of interest. There was an increase in aimed funds whereas there was an insignificant decline in borrowings. The index of non-interest income in the total income was continuously increasing.

Belay *et al.* (2004)[24] found that there is a six fold time increase in amount of deposits in Primary Agricultural Credit Societies. The magnitude of deposit, mobilized per society increased by more than four times over the study period. The analysis of the composition of working capital infers that the societies were highly dependent upon the external financial sources mainly borrowings. The share of owned funds to the total working capital was very small. The absolute amount of loans advanced increased considerably over time. The share of term loans advanced accounted more than 95 per cent of the total agricultural loans advanced.

Chellani and Rai (2004)[25] analysed the performance of District Central Cooperative Banks in Gujarat. They found that the deposits constitute a large share of working funds of all banking organisations. A high share reflects their autonomy in the intermediation process. The higher dependence of DCCBs on institutional source of deposits reveals the lack of aggressive marketing outlook in canvassing low cost deposits from individuals. The recovery performance in Gujarat State is not only poor but also reveals a substantial temporal decline compared to the All India level.

Prasad (2004)[26] identified the reasons for poor performance of urban co-operative banks. They are lack of banking knowledge among the members of staff, political factors, lack of valuation of mortgaged property of borrowers, sanction of loans against Patta lands, purpose of loans, very narrow margins, non-conduct of periodical inspection, improper valuation of assets/securities mortgaged, improper investment in Government securities and other approved securities/bonds and lack of training to staff and to members of management board.

Avinash (2004)[27] compared the performance of urban co-operative banks in pre-reform period and post-reform period. The linear growth rate of membership in post-reform period is lower than the pre-reform period. The compound growth rate of share capital is identified as higher in pre-reform period whereas regarding the own fund, the compound growth rate in post-reform period is less. Regarding deposits, the higher compound growth rate is observed in post-reform period whereas in loans and advances, the compound growth rate is much less.

Kulandaiswamy and Murugesan (2004)[28] used eight parameters to measure the performance of Primary Agricultural Credit Societies. Out of the 30 societies, only 23.3 per cent showed a good performance whereas 40 per cent revealed moderate performance. The eight parameters used to evaluate the performance are working capital, total loan outstanding, total business turnover overdues, net worth, subsidies and grants, net profits and loans to weaker sections.

Koteshwara Rao and Chandran (2005)[29] used the linear, second degree parabola and exponential curve to analyse the performance of consumer cooperative stores in Andhra Pradesh. They confirmed the straight line is more appropriate to represent sales data. By that, they concluded that the annual growth rate of sales in the super Bazar is 90.7274.

Suhag *et al.* (2005)[30] found the performance of Primary Agricultural Co-operative Credit Societies in Haryana. He revealed that all villages in the State are covered by the PACSs. The compound growth rate of membership is 5.29 per cent. The compound growth rates for agricultural and non-agricultural loan during the study period are 22.06 and 32.46 per cent respectively. The percentage of defaulters to total members indicates that the overdues was the serious problem of the PACs over the span of the study period.

Teli (2005)[31] identified the performance of urban co-operative banks in Kolhapur district. From the foregoing analysis, the progress of different indicators of UCBs in the district showed a considerable growth in their membership, share capital, reserves, owned funds, deposits, loans and net profits. But at the same time increase in overdues and number of banks making losses reflected an urgent need for further investigation of the working of the UCBs in Kop district.

Junare (2005)[32] evaluated the performance of urban co-operative bank. The important criterion for judging the efficiency of bank is its profitability, the share capital, the level of advances and growth of membership.

Jadhav and Kasar (2006)[33] used the performance index to measure the performance of District Central Co-operative Banks in Maharashtra. The performance index indicates that one third of the banks in Maharashtra were the strong units among 30 District Central Co-operative Banks since the respective performance index were greater than 6.0 whereas five DCCBs were very poor in their performance since the respective performance index were less than 1.00.

Patil (2006)[34] analysed the financial and operational performance of non-agricultural co-operative credit societies. The financial performance was revealed with the help of paid up capital per member, deposit per member, advances per member, overdue percentage and credit deposit ratio. The operational performance was evaluated with the help of interest to deployed fund, total income to deployed fund, total expenses to total income, interest, expenses to total income, interest expenses to interest income, non-interest expenses to interest income, staff expenses to total income, net profit to working capital and net profit to total income ratio.

Viability of Co-operative Societies

Bhattacharjee (1999)[35] revealed that the total gross margin is the most important route for increasing the profitability of the co-operatives. The evidence on scale economies suggests that the Primary Agricultural Co-operative Societies (PACS) have not exploited the potential for expansion and viability fully. It may be due to centralized and bureaucratic decision-making in its vertically integrated three tier structure. Restraint on increases in both tending and deposit interest rates is required so that the PACS can expand to fully exploit the scale economies in costs that they have.

Devaraja (1999)[36] discussed the economic viability of co-operative central bank. The economic viability was analysed with the help of demand, collection and overdues. By analysis he concluded that the overdue to demand was declining during the study period. The drastic cut in the agricultural credit during the study period indicates the banks' diversification of credit portfolio. The cost of management was increasing faster than the return from the credit.

Subburaj and Karunakaran (2002)[37] studied the trend of urban cooperative banks in Tamil Nadu and India. The compound growth rate of number of banks in Tamil Nadu is negative whereas in India, it is positive. The compound growth rates in membership, paid up capital, reserves, deposits, borrowings and working capital in India are greater than those in Tamil Nadu.

Shah (2002)[38] found that the financial viability of the credit societies is seen to have improved during the post-economic reform period as compared to pre-economic reform period since it could achieve break even levels of advance plus deposits and assets plus liabilities much earlier during the latter period as compared to the former period. The margin money per hundred rupee of loan advance plus deposits declined because of increase in variable cost per hundred rupee of loan advance plus deposits.

Masali (2004)[39] analysed the viability of banks with the help of the parameters namely the weighted average cost of resources, weighted average earning of assets, financial margin cost of management and employee efficiency. He concluded that the urban cooperative banks in Belgaum suffered by absence of large branch network, small area of operation, absence of training and expertise to the staff and management, competition from co-operative credit societies, private banks and nationalised commercial banks; and delay in decision-making.

Zakir Hussain (2005)[40] analysed the viability of State Co-operative Banks in Kerala. He revealed that the loss scenario of SCBs is seen on the higher side. Even though, the SCBs showed a good signal on deposit mobilisation and highest loan disbursement, their loss scenario is a discouraging signal. The important reasons for the loss are the high establishment cost and the increase in overdues. Most of the branches were identified as operating even less than their break even level of operations.

Nayak (2004)[41] identified that the cooperatives constitute the sub-structure upon which the super structure of State economy is founded. Any structural change of super structure is bound to have its ramification on the functioning of sub-structure. Yet, the strength of super structure depends upon the strength of sub-structure. Cooperatives are the effective mechanism of structural change.

Attitude of Members and Employees of Co-operative Societies

Sivaprahasam (2000)[42] found that there is a decline in the overdues position of the cooperative societies in the recent years. There is a steady increase in the average net profit earned by the societies during the study period. The important reasons why persons working in the societies do not prefer to continue for more number of years might be inadequate salary in commensurate with their educational qualification. The employees are not well paid despite the scope for higher pay structure.

Sarangi and Raman (2000)[43] indicated that six variables discriminate the members from non-members regarding their attitude towards consumer co-operative stores. They include the social benefits of co-operatives, human qualities in co-operatives and leadership development in co-operative organisations. The important reasons to prefer co-operative organisations are participation in management, self improvement, self-respect and self fulfilment.

Das (2002)[44] revealed the utilisation pattern of cooperative credit among the borrowers. The misutilisation in the form of diversification of loans has become a common problem. The main reasons for the diversification are poor economic conditions of borrowers, lack of proper supervision, indebtedness of borrowers and wrong identification of borrowers. It can be concluded from the analysis that improper utilisation of loans and the insignificant repayment behaviour have stood on the way of the development process of rural sector. To have the utilisation of loans in proper manner, the bank should take utmost care in identifying borrowers, pre-sanction feasibility study and post sanction follow-up measures.

Junare (2002)[45] pointed out the importance of customer oriented approach in cooperative banks. He identified the following expectations from banks: expeditious decisions in disposal of requests made by the customers, prompt attention and efficient service across the counter, speedy attendance to the customer requests, accuracy of information provided by the bank, transparency in banker customer relationships, assurance of legitimate secrecy of customer operations, availability of advice and consultancy whenever the customer requires, equitable treatment, customer education about the banking schemes and simplified procedures.

Rao (2002)[46] attempted to study the socio-economic profile of users of urban cooperative banks in Bangalore city. Most of the customers are in the age of 31-50 years and belong to the working class. Average distance between the bank and the residences of the respondents is 1 to 5 kilometres. Majority of the respondents are happy in the sciences of the banks.

Rao (2002)[47] found that majority of the employees liked co-operatives and they believed in the ideology of co-operation. The important perceived facilities availed of from the societies are festival advance, vehicle advance and leave encashment facilities. The highly expected facilities from the societies are leave travel concessions, reimbursement of family medical expenses and loans for constructions of houses. The least expected services from the societies are voluntary retirement, mortgage loan, employees' sports and cultural activities fund and housing quarters.

Rao (2003)[48] discussed the employees' attitudes towards cooperatives and facilities in urban co-operative banks. He found that the employees were highly dissatisfied with the service offered by the co-operatives. They are dissatisfied with the behaviour of employees at co-operative banks. They had rated the facilities at the banks were not competitive.

Vimala (2004)[49] analysed the customer service in cooperatives. She revealed that majority of the customers are satisfied and highly satisfied with the customer service in cooperatives. The highly perceived aspects among the customers are guidance and promptness, and the behaviour of the employees. The dissatisfied aspects among the customers are the present facilities at banks.

Natarajan and Murugesan (2004)[50] revealed that the greatest strength of the co-operative stores is increase in sales and purchases. The main weaknesses are lack of after sales service, high manpower and establishment expenses, higher degree of wastages. The opportunities are the chances for the development and effective utilisation whereas the threats are competition, high salary increase, high wastage, high storing cost, bad debts and rules and regulations.

Problems and Prospects of Co-operative Societies

Satish and Deshpande (1999)[51] focussed the challenges faced by the co-operative banks. These are facing competition, need for Human Resource Development for new areas, viable interest rate for deposits and loans, change of view on cost of funds, business risk, minimum break even rate required, developing the sensitivity among top management, introduction of technologies and competence building among the staff.

Varkey (1996)[52] stated that the team spirit developed through personal inter-action and training has enabled the society to acquire faster growth in spite of very stiff competition in its areas of operation. The importance given by the management to training is quite laudable and this has proved its results in its operations.

Lotoria *et al.* (2000)[53] identified the factors associated with the repayment position of agricultural credit user. They are education, caste, size of holding, annual income, size of family, contact with extension agents, availability of irrigation, availability of loan and attitude towards co-operative societies. Further it could be concluded that the coefficient to borrowed loan showed a positive and significant relationship with overdues in all the size groups. The factors responsible for regular repayment are good crop with remunerative price and auction.

Srinath[54] (2001) found the reasons for deterioration in the co-operative banking system. These are the level of overdues, deregulated rate of interest, lack of diversification, interference of State Governments, credit limit imposed by the National Board for Agriculture and Rural Development, lack of refinancing facilities, lack of training of staff in run-farm finance and housing financing.

Devaraja (2001)[55] found that the Mahila Co-operative Bank Ltd., Karnataka had made good progress, particularly in share capital. Deposits constitute one of the important source of funds for its operations. The bank has failed to comply with social services interests of its members. Although the objective of the bank is to enter into participation arrangements with other banks or financial institutions with the object of making more loans, the bank has not made any effort in this direction.

Veera Kumaran and Subash (2001)[56] identified the most important feature of Palakkad urban co-operative bank limited is that the bank had not borrowed any funds from any of the financial agencies. The proportion of fixed deposits to total deposits is increasing over a period of time when the savings deposits and current deposits show a declining picture. It clearly reflects the non-participation of business community in the activities of the bank. The decrease in percentage of credit to working capital and deposits indicates lack of scientific portfolio management.

Shah (2001)[57] identified that there is a considerable increase in the membership, share capital, owned funds, deposits, working capital and loan advancement in the Primary Agricultural Co-operative Credit Societies in Maharashtra. Many deficiencies have been identified in the functioning of these societies especially in its operational efficiency. The low operational efficiency is caused by high incidence of overdues, low level of recovery, distributional aspects of short term and medium term loans and coverage of scheduled caste and scheduled tribe members.

Goswami and Hazarika (2002)[58] identified that the problems in consumer cooperatives are varied in nature. A few dominant problems of the CCS are undue government interference, weak financial status, inefficient stock and sales management, human resource problem and unhealthy competition with private traders. The private establishments provide day-long sales service without break whereas the CCS is opened for few hours and closed according to scheduled time with tea-break, lunch-break, holidays, etc. Besides, the cooperatives work like a government department and not like a business enterprise.

Sarhar (2002)[59] identified that the problems of the weavers' co-operative societies in Maharashtra are dormancy, encroachment of intermediaries, low accessibility of raw-materials, limiting production and disposal problems, unfair competition, marketing and infrastructural problems, obsolete technology, lack of working capital, lack of training facilities, lack of promotion and publicity and proper incentives.

Chidambaram and Ganesan (2002)[60] classified the defaulters as genuine defaulters and wilful defaulters. The important causes for default among the genuine defaulters are inadequate income generation, crop failure, heavy expenditure on social ceremonies, misuse of loan, short duration of repayment period and others. The reasons for wilful default are the direction from the farmers' association, the over sympathetic treatment of the government towards defaulters and the influence of political leaders. The profile variables namely sex, marital status, literacy level, size of family, household income and land holdings are statistically associated with the amount of overdues.

Sen *et al.* (2002)[61] found that the co-operative enterprises of the Morang district may be gripped by serious state of sickness. The causes for that sickness are frequent changes in government policy, problems of availability of raw materials, power, skilled labour, poor management, decline in capacity utilisation and decline in quality of products and services. The persistent shortage of cash and default in payment to suppliers, employees, banks, etc., have appeared to be the important symptoms of financial sickness.

Thirupurasundari (2003)[62] examined the problems of overdues in co-operative housing societies. She revealed that there is no significant relationship between the age of the borrowers and the number of defaulters and there is also no significant relationship between the income of the member and the number of defaulters. It is found that the defaulters are more in case of urban societies and taluk society. In the case of urban societies the defaulters are more in the age group of 46-55 while in the case of taluk society the defaulters are more in the age group of 36 to 45.

Thiruthuvadoss (2004)[63] used the multiple regression analysis to examine the determinants of profit in District Central Cooperative Banks. The profit determinants in the case of Trichirappalli DCCB are reserve fund, working capital and overdues. All these determinants are inversely related to profits. In the case of Kancheepuram DCCB, the important profit determinants are the reserve fund, working capital, overdues and number of branches.

Ramesh (2005)[64] identified a continuous loss in credit co-operatives. He also identified the steep increase in the management cost. The important reasons for that losses were identified as the flow in utilization of loans, lack of professionalism, lack of innovative financial resource management, political entanglement, lack of consumption loans and the proper assessment of credit needs.

Teli (2004)[65] revealed the important problems faced by urban cooperative banks in India. These are duel control, untrained human capital, limited area of operation, lack of marketing view, limited resources, lack of proper support from the government, problem of recovery, low computerization, lack of transparency, in complete corporate governance and lack of conceptual awareness.

Taori (2005)[66] identified that some precautionary measures to avoid financial crisis in urban co-operative banks. These are Management of Human Resources, application of systems and procedures, manual of instructions on systems and procedures; audit and inspection/concurrent audit, professionalisation; meaning and development, effective deployment of funds, investments, rate of interest and credit portfolio.

Zahir Hussain (2005)[67] identified the poor repayment in cooperative banks is attributed to a number of reasons such as poor identification of purpose of loan, sanctioning of loan for non-productive purpose and poor monitoring in the utilisation of loan. The mobilisation of deposits without planning for its proper disposal, puts the banks in paying interest for the idle funds. The higher establishment cost ends with incurrent loss. In total, the banks are experiencing high competition.

Annamalai and Bhuvaneswari (2005)[68] identified that there are several positive developments pertaining to balance sheets, profits and income and asset quality of urban co-operative banks.

The net profit of the scheduled UCBs shows a substantial growth of 40.4 per cent while the net loss of UCBs declines by 69.1 per cent. It is also recorded a modest decline in non-performing assets both in absolute as well as in percentage terms. The decline in NPAs is higher due to increased provisioning.

Mishra and Pattanaik (2005)[69] examined the relative contribution of factors responsible for increasing overdues of farmers. The amount of overdue is highly influenced by the consumption expenditure, repaying capacity and cropping intensity. The significantly influencing factors on overdues among wilful defaulters are operational size of holdings and size of loan whereas among the non-wilful defaulters, these factors are size of loan and consumption expenditure.

Thirupurasundari (2006)[70] identified the important problems faced by the co-operative housing societies. These are inadequate finance, delay in sanctioning loan, problem of overdues and continuous losses. It was found that the seasonal crop failure, monsoon failure, unexpected expenses due to domestic and religious functions are the important reasons for the problem of overdues.

SUMMARY

The above said reviews examined the performance of cooperatives, banks and societies, the customer's and employee's perception on the services offered by the banks and societies. The problems encountered by the customers and staff were discussed. The nature of default and the reasons for default among the customers were analysed. Even though there are so many studies related to the performance evaluation of the cooperative banks and societies, only a few studies are related to the Employee Cooperative Thrift and Credit Societies (ECTCS). But those few studies also present a bird view on the working of ECTCS. So that the present study focus on an indepth analysis on ECTCS at three different dimensions namely performance appraisal, members' view on ECTCS and the staff's view on them.

REFERENCES

1. Suhag, K.S., Goyal, S.K., and Grora, R.K., "The Performance of Co-operative Credit Institutions in Haryana", *Indian Co-operative Review,* 35(4), April 1998, pp. 323-336.

2. Narasimha Reddy, S., Jayarama, Srinivasa, G., Lekshmana, S., and Gethadevi, R.G., "Performance of Silk Handloom Weavers' Co-operative Societies in Andhra Pradesh – A Financial Performance", *Indian Co-operative Review,* 4(2), July 1998, pp.44-51.

3. Asthana, A.K., and Manali Phatak, "Marketing of Loans/Advances in Urban Co-operative Banks", *Agricultural Banker,* 23(1), January-March 1999, pp. 39-45.

4. Devaraja, T.S., "Working of District Central Co-operative Bank, Hassan, Karnataka: An Analysis", *Indian Co-operative Review,* 35(3), January 1999, pp. 263-270.

5. Devaraja, T.S., "An Evaluation of Bee-keepers Cooperative Society Limited, Sahleshpur [Hassan District, Karnataka]", *Cooperative Perspective,* 34(1), April-June 1999, pp. 47-50.

6. Padmini, E.V.K., and Jaish, P.C., "Financial Performance of Regional Rural Banks — A Case Study of the North Malabar Gramin Bank", *Agricultural Banker,* 23(3), July-September 1999, pp. 39-48.

7. Subbiah, A., "Deposits, Loans Issued on Recovery Performance of Central Cooperative Banks in India", *Tamil Nadu Journal of Cooperation,* 91(6), September 1999, pp. 49-51.

8. Deepak B. Bhamare and Agarwal, V.S., "A Study of the Capital Structure of Dairy Co-operatives in Maharashtra: A Case Study Related to Dhule District", *The Maharashtra Co-operative Quarterly,* 83(2), October-December 1999, pp. 57-64.

9. Dinesh Singh Yadav, "Performance and Prospects of Agricultural Cooperative Credit Societies in Block Bilhaur District Kanpur – Dehak (U.P)", *Indian Cooperative Review,* 37(2), October 1999, pp. 74-77.

10. Dash, D.K., "Financial Performance Evaluation through Ratio Analysis — A Case Study of Nawanajar Cooperative Bank", Jamnagar (Gujarat)", *Indian Cooperative Review,* 37(3), January 2000, pp. 162-170.

11. Padmini, E.V.K., "Trends in Pattern of Sources and Uses of Funds of District Co-operative Banks in Kerala", *Co-operative Perspective,* 34(4), January-March 2000, pp. 7-14.

12. Sukhdev Singh and Maninder Kaur, "Performance of Agricultural Cooperative Service Societies in Punjab: An Appraisal", *Cooperative Perspective,* 34(4), January-March 2000, pp. 16-25.

13. Teli, R.B., "Performance Evaluation of Urban Co-operative Banks in Kolhapur District", *The Maharashtra Co-operative Quarterly*, 98(1), April-June 2006, pp. 34-36.

14. Krishna Rao, G.V., Chandra Shekhar and Narender, I., "Growth Analysis — A Critical Review of the Karimnagar District Cooperative Central Bank (KDCCB) Andhra Pradesh", *Indian Cooperative Review*, 38(1), July 2000, pp. 21-29.

15. Masthan, D., and Narayanasamy, R., "Financial Analysis of Chittoor Co-operative Town Bank", *Co-operative Perspective*, 35(3), October-December 2000, pp. 87-94.

16. Lopoyelum Samwel Kakuko, "A Micro-analysis of the Cost of Default and Evaluation of Primary Agricultural Co-operative Banks (PACBs) — A Case of Rural Financing", Co-operative Perspective, 35(3), October-December 2000, pp. 51-65.

17. Kumar Rajitha, "Working of Urban Cooperative Banks — A Case Study", The Maharashtra Co-operative Quarterly, 84(4) April-June 2001, pp. 53-59.

18. Rengasamy, V., "Factors Influencing Profitability of the Melur Co-operative Urban Bank An Analysis", *Tamil Nadu Journal of Co-operation*, 1(8), June 2001, pp. 45-47.

19. Ali Ashraf and Banahar Basavaraja, "Performance of Co-operative Oil Mills in Karnataka — A Management Appraisal", *Indian Co-operative Review*, 11(3), October 2001, pp. 102-113.

20. Sahayoga, "The Role of Cooperative in Reducing Regional Imbalances in Karnataka", Report Submitted to the High Power Committee for *Redressal of Regional Imbalances, Government of Karnataka*, June 2002.

21. Raihar, A.V., "Growth, Profitability and Cost Efficiency of Urban Co-operative Banks in India: A Comparative Analysis", *Indian Co-operative Review*, 40(2), October 2002, pp. 117-124.

22 Hussain Zahir, "Malabar's Pride: Performance Evaluation of the Malappuram District Central Cooperative Bank Ltd.", *Cooperative Perspective*, 38(2), July-September 2003, pp. 42-46.

23. Dayanandan, R., and Sasikumar, K., "Performance Evaluation of District Co-operative Banks of Kerala", *Indian Co-operative Review*, 46(2), October, 2003, pp. 102-109.

24. Belay Ayenew, Suhag, K.S., and Arun Kumar, "The Performance of Primary Agricultural Co-operative Credit Societies in Haryana", *Indian Co-operative Review*, 41(4), April 2004, pp. 246-261.

25. Chellani, D.K., and Rai Rita, "The Performance of District Central Cooperative Banks in Gujarat", *Indian Cooperative Review*, 41(4), April 2004, pp. 289-296.

26. Prasad Ravi, S., "Performance of Urban Co-operative Banks — Some Aspects", *The Co-operator*, 41(10), April 2004, pp. 411-414.

27. Raikan Avinash, V., "Performance, Problems and Prospects of the Urban Co-operative Banks in Goa", *Indian Co-operative Review*, 42(2), October 2004, pp. 183-195.

28. Kulandaiswamy, V., and Murugesan, P., "Performance of PACS — An Empirical Evaluation", *Indian Co-operative Review*, 42(2), October 2004, pp. 121-130.

29. Koteswara Rao, M., and Chandran, K., "Performance of Consumer Cooperative Stores in Andhra Pradesh: A Case Study of Vijayakrishna Super Bazar, Vijayawada", *Indian Cooperative Review*, 42(4), April 2005, pp. 341-349.

30. Suhag, K.S., Parminder Malik and Arun Kumar, "Performance of Primary Agricultural Co-operative Credit Societies in Haryana", *Indian Economic Panorama*, 15(2), July 2005, pp. 51-53.

31 Teli, R.B., "Performance Evaluation of Urban Co-operative Banks in Kolhapur District", *Indian Co-operative Review*, 43(1), July 2005, pp. 457-459.

32. Junare, S.O., "Role of Urban Cooperative Banks in Financing of Primity and Weaker Sector in Gujarat", *National Institute of Co-operative Management*, Bulletin, September 2005, p. 3.

33. Jadhav, K.L., and Kasar, D.V., "Performance of District Central Co-operative Banks in Maharashtra: A Model for Quantitative Analysis", *The Maharashtra Co-operative Quarterly*, 101(4), January-March 2006, pp. 37-43.

34. Patil, K.V., "Evaluation of Financial Working and Operational Performance of Non-Agricultural Credit Societies in Jalagon District with Special Reference to Panola City", *The Maharashtra Co-operative Quarterly*, 98(1), April-June 2006, pp. 21-26.

35. Bhattacharjee, Sourindra, "Factors Influencing Viability of Primary Agricultural Co-operative Credit Societies", *Prajnan*, 27(1), 1999, pp. 29-34.

36. Devaraja, T.S., "An Analysis of Working of District Co-operative Central Bank, Hassan, Karnataka", *The Maharashtra Quarterly*, 83(2), October-December 1999, pp. 49-56.

37. Subburaj, B., and Karunakaran, P., "Adoption of Modern Strategies by Urban Co-operative Banks in Tamil Nadu", *Indian Co-operative Review*, 29(3), January 2002, pp. 227-233.

38. Shah, Deepak, "How far Credit Co-operatives Viable in the New Economic Environment: An Evidence from Maharashtra", *Prajnan*, 30(2), 2002, pp. 149-174.

39. Masali, S.S., "The Performance of Cooperative Urban Banks: A Study of Cooperative Urban Banks in Belgaum", *Indian Cooperative Review*, 42(1), July 2004, pp. 64-71.

40. Hussain, Zakir, A.K., "Status of Service Co-operative Banks in Kerala", *The Co-operator*, 42(11), May 2005, pp. 472-476.

41. Nayak, Sri Sudarsan, "Cooperative — The Vehicle of Economic Growth with Specific reference to Orissa", *Indian Cooperative Review*, 42(1), July 2004, pp. 83-85.

42. Sivaprahasam, P., "Working of the Employees Cooperative Credit Societies in Tamil Nadu", *Tamil Nadu Journal of Cooperation*, 91(10), January 2000, pp. 53-58.

43. Sarangi, Mrutyunjay and Raman, M., "Discriminant Analysis of Members and Non-Members' Perception Towards Consumer Co-operatives in Tamil Nadu", *Co-operative Perspective*, 35(3), October-December 2000, pp. 14-29.

44. Das, Debrata, "Utilisation Pattern of Cooperative Credit: A Case Study", *Cooperative Perspective*, 36(4), January-March 2002, pp. 23-28.

45. Junare, S.O., "Customer Oriented Approach in Cooperative Banks", *Cooperative Perspective*, 37(1), April-June 2002, pp. 33-36.

46. Rao, Akula Rajagopala, "Socio-Economic Profile of Customers' Service in Urban Cooperative Banks: A Study", *Cooperative Perspective*, 31(2), July-September 2002, pp. 60-67.

47. Rao, Akula Rajagopala, "Employees' Attitudes Towards Co-operatives and Facilities in Urban Co-operative Banks: A Study", *Indian Co-operative Review*, 40(2), October 2002, pp. 108-118.

48. Rao, Akula Rajagopala, "Employees' Attitude Towards Co-operatives and Facilities in Urban Co-operative Banks: A Case Study", *Indian Co-operative Review*, 40(2), October 2003, pp. 107-113.

49. Vimala, P., "Customer Service in Cooperatives", *Indian Co-operative Review*, 41(4), April 2004, pp. 284-288.

50. Natarajan, P., and Murugesan, M., "Services of Employees Cooperative Stores – Members' Perception", *Tamil Nadu Journal of Cooperation*, 4(11), September 2004, pp. 27-30.

51. Satish, P. and Deshpande, D.V., "Co-operative Banks and Regional Rural Banks: The Challenges Ahead", *Agricultural Banker*, 23(3), July-September 1999, pp. 27-31.

52. Varkey, V.O., "An Urban Credit Society's Progress and Training Outlook", *The Maharashtra Co-operative Quarterly*, 80(4), January-March 1996, pp. 1-5.

53. Lotoria, S.K., Jauloar, A.M., Daipuria, O.P., and Sharma, S.K., "An Analysis of Overdues and Repayment Behaviour of Agricultural Credit (A Case Study of Gwaliar District)", *Land Bank Journal*, December 2000, pp. 45-50.

54. Srinath, A.R., "Co-operative Credit in India – Problems and Suggestions", *Indian Consumer Co-operator*, 28 (2), April-June 2001, pp. 11-13.

55. Devaraja, T.S., "Performance Evaluation of Sarada Mahila Co-operative Bank Ltd., in Mysore City of Karnataka", *The Maharashtra Co-operative Quarterly*, 84(4), April-June 2001, pp. 31-40.

56. Veera Kumaran, G., and Subash, B., "The Palakkad Urban Co-operative Bank Limited — A Case Study", *Indian Co-operative Review*, 37(4), April 2001, pp. 255-264.

57. Shah, Deepak, "Primary Agricultural Co-operative Credit Societies in Maharashtra: Some Emerging Issues", *Prajnan*, 29(1), 2001, pp. 31-51.

58. Goswani, H., and Hazarika, P., "Problems and Prospects of Consumer Cooperatives in Assam in the New Millennium", *Indian Cooperative Review*, 39(4), April 2002, pp. 295-307.

59. Sarhar, A.N., "Problems and Prospects of Weavers' Co-operative Societies in Maharashtra", *Co-operative Perspective*, 37(2), July-September 2002, pp. 31-46.

60. Chidambaram, K., and Ganesan, S., "Overdues in Primary Agricultural Cooperative Banks in Madurai District: A Study", Cooperative Perspective, 37(3), October-December 2002, pp. 58-63.

61. Sen, Dilip Kumar, Jain, Sugan C. and Bala, Swapan Kumar, "Financial Sickness of Co-operative Organisations in Morang District", *Indian Journal of Accounting*, 33(6), December 2002, pp. 1-6.

62. Thiripurasundari, K., "Problems of Overdues in Co-operative Housing Societies — A Case Study", *Indian Co-operative Review*, 41(1), July 2003, pp. 53-63.

63. Thiruthuvadoss, S.P., "Determinants of Profit in District Central Cooperative Banks", *Tamil Nadu Journal of Cooperation*, 4(5), March 2004, pp. 21-23.

64. Ramesh, D., "Restructuring of Credit Co-operatives: An Issue of Imperative Need", *The Maharashtra Co-operative Quarterly*, 97(12), January-March 2005, pp. 17-25.

65. Teli, R.B., "An Evaluation of the Working of Urban Cooperative Banking in India — Problems and Prospects", *Indian Cooperative Review*, 42(1), July 2004, pp. 85-95.

66. Taori, V.K., "An Analytical View on Urban Co-operative Banks", *The Co-operator*, 42(10), April 2005, pp. 411-416.

67. Zahir Hussain, A.K., "Problems and Prospects of Service Cooperative Banks in Kerala", *Tamil Nadu Journal of Cooperation*, 5(7), May 2005, pp. 23-25.

68. Annamalai, S., and Bhuvaneswari, P., "Urban Cooperative Banks poised for Growth", *Tamil Nadu Journal of Cooperation*, 5(11), September 2005, pp. 30-32.

69. Mishra, R.K., and Pattanaik, S., "Repayment Performance of Borrowers with Respect to Agricultural Loans on Khruda Block of Khunda block of Khunda District, Orissa", *Indian Co-operative Review*, 43(1), July 2005, pp. 423-441.

70. Thirupurasundari, K., "Problems of the Co-operative Housing Societies — A Case Analysis", *The Co-operator*, 439(7), January 2006, pp. 321-325.

3

FINANCIAL PERFORMANCE OF EMPLOYEES CO-OPERATIVE THRIFT AND CREDIT SOCIETIES

INTRODUCTION

The financial performance of ECTCS in Kanyakumari district is analysed with the help of the financial statement analysis. The financial statements reflect the state of affairs of an organisation at a given point of time as well as its financial performance over a period. However, the accounting figures disclosed in the financial statement cannot be claimed as a true financial indicator of a firm's performance. Sometimes it is alluring to picture illusion figures in Balance Sheet or Income Statement, but after a detailed analysis, the study may end up with dismal performance. Thus, there is a need to analyse the financial statements by determining the relationship between two figures. This is ascertained by a technique called Ratio Analysis which expresses the numerical relationship between two mean values of accounting figures.

FINANCIAL AND OPERATIONAL INDICATORS

In the present study, the performance of the ECTCS in Kanyakumari District is exhibited with the help of the mean values of various financial and operational indicators of 23 societies of Nagercoil Division and 13 societies of Thuckalay division. The annual and compound growth rates of the indicators have been computed.

The Mean Values of Number of Members and Share Capital of the Societies

The mean values of number of members and share capital of the societies at Nagercoil and Thuckalay have been computed and presented in Table 3.1.

Table 3.1

Average of Number of Members and Average of Share Capital of the Societies

Year	*Societies at Nagercoil*		*Societies at Thuckalay*	
	Mean of Number of Members	*Mean of Share Capital (Rs.)*	*Mean of Number of Members*	*Mean of Share Capital (Rs.)*
1994-95	734.70	14,79,360	698.08	9,93,904
1995-96	747.39	16,54,062	843.71	12,92,971
1996-97	748.04	19,32,840	929.54	18,78,559
1997-98	755.48	22,63,316	984.92	23,58,596
1998-99	772.26	27,02,905	1026.69	27,65,159
1999-00	765.26	32,12,071	1068.85	32,27,089
2000-01	758.00	36,66,016	1056.15	34,82,966
2001-02	729.26	38,96,762	1033.08	35,02,370
2002-03	702.00	40,49,704	1022.54	35,93,478
2003-04	673.87	42,84,175	982.38	35,95,653
AGR	–0.5791*	0.9918*	0.7322*	0.9545*
CGR (in percentage)	–0.81	13.55	3.20	15.07

* Significant at 5 per cent level.
AGR – Annual Growth Rate
CGR – Compound Growth Rate

The average of number of members of the societies at Nagercoil was increasing from 734.7 in 1994-95 to 772.26 in 1998-99 and then it was gradually declining to 673.87 in 2003-04. The average of share capital was increasing from Rs. 14.79 lakh to Rs. 42.84 lakh.

The average of number of members of the societies at Thuckalay was increasing from 698.08 in 1994-95 to 1068-85 in 1999-00 and then it was decreasing to 982.38 in 2003-04. The average of share capital was increasing from Rs.9.94 lakh to Rs. 35.95 lakh.

The compound growth rates of members of the societies at Nagercoil and Thuckalay were –0.81 per cent and 3.2 per cent respectively and the compound growth rates of share capital were 13.55 and 15.07 per cent respectively.

Deposits and Loans Disbursed by the Societies

The deposits of the societies are collected from the members in the form of recurring deposits and fixed deposits. The loans are disbursed by the societies to their members on the basis of their repaying capacity. Generally, only medium term loans are granted to the members. Since, the main activities of the financial organisations are receiving of deposits and lending of loans, the present study has made an attempt to analyse the mean values of deposits of the societies at Nagercoil and Thuckalay. The growth rate of deposits is also computed to exhibit the overall trend of deposits of the societies. Similarly, the mean of loans disbursed by the societies is computed. The resulted mean values and the compound growth rates of deposits and loans are exhibited in Table 3.2.

The mean of deposits of the societies at Nagercoil was increasing from Rs. 24.92 lakh in 1994-95 to Rs. 87.44 lakh in 2003-04. The compound growth rate of the deposits during the study period was 9.93 per cent. The average of loans disbursed by the societies was increasing from Rs. 39.25 lakh in 1994-95 to Rs. 104.51 lakh in 2003-04 whereas their compound growth rate was 12.43 per cent.

Table 3.2

Mean Values of Deposits and Loans Disbursed by the Societies

Year	*Societies at Nagercoil*		*Societies at Thuckalay*	
	Deposits (Rs.)	*Loans (Rs.)*	*Deposits (Rs.)*	*Loans (Rs.)*
1994-95	24,92,104	39,24,702	6,58,305	26,45,844
1995-96	28,72,356	39,12,401	9,24,586	34,73,262
1996-97	33,30,128	45,50,322	12,92,364	42,38,762
1997-98	38,95,535	55,22,093	17,01,119	55,21,780
1998-99	44,77,524	64,56,811	22,28,767	57,88,351
1999-00	52,68,129	74,99,590	26,97,835	78,06,230
2000-01	61,73,920	81,43,041	32,01,170	67,91,702
2001-02	71,67,667	85,16,153	35,07,396	88,08,524
2002-03	79,68,668	93,17,040	36,51,022	75,55,646
2003-04	87,43,700	1,04,51,155	38,50,130	1,15,32,407
AGR	0.7997*	0.9934*	0.9914*	0.9437*
CGR (in per cent)	9.93	12.43	21.84	15.14

* Significant at 5 per cent level. AGR – Annual Growth Rate. CGR – Compound Growth Rate.

In the case of the Thuckalay societies, mean of deposits was increasing from Rs. 6.58 lakh in 1994-95 to Rs. 38.50 lakh in 2003-04. The compound growth rate of deposits was 21.84 per cent. The average of loan disbursed was increasing from Rs. 26.46 lakh to Rs. 115.32 lakh and the compound growth rate was 15.14 per cent. The analysis reveals that the means of deposits of the societies at Nagercoil was greater whereas the mean of loans disbursed by the societies at Thuckalay was greater when the two division societies were compared.

Spread of the Societies

The spread indicates the difference between interest received and interest paid. It reveals the operational gain of the societies. Since the societies have borrowed funds from different sources, they have to pay the interest. At the same time, the societies receive interest from the members who have borrowed loans. The increase in spread will increase the profit of the concern. The important reason for the increase in spread is dispersal of large amount of loan which will increase the amount of interest received. Higher the difference between the interest received and interest paid the higher will be the profit of the societies and it indicates the credit worthiness of the societies. So it is very essential to include the interest received, interest paid and spread. In the present study, the mean values of interest received, interest paid and the spread of the societies from 1994-95 to 2003-04 have been calculated and shown in Table 3.3.

Table 3.3

Mean Values of Interest Received, Paid and Spread of the Societies

Year	*Societies at Nagercoil*			*Societies at Thuckalay*		
	Interest Received (Rs.)	*Interest Paid (Rs.)*	*Spread (Rs.)*	*Interest Received (Rs.)*	*Interest Paid (Rs.)*	*Spread (Rs.)*
1994-95	6,09,324	2,91,030	3,18,294	5,03,966	2,80,386	2,23,580
1995-96	7,18,712	3,53,123	3,65,589	7,52,261	4,73,974	2,78,284
1996-97	8,15,447	4,07,443	4,08,004	11,22,956	6,97,788	4,25,168
1997-98	10,05,096	5,07,701	4,97,395	15,51,142	11,11,125	4,40,017
1998-99	11,37,952	5,93,804	5,44,148	17,71,739	10,99,856	6,71,883
1999-00	13,77,290	7,16,840	6,60,450	18,61,068	10,74,464	7,86,604
2000-01	15,55,090	8,04,640	7,50,450	19,84,465	11,22,785	8,61,680
2001-02	17,34,098	9,20,216	8,13,882	22,20,006	12,30,525	9,89,481
2002-03	19,95,133	10,34,214	9,60,919	22,91,470	16,17,874	6,73,596
2003-04	17,27,788	10,21,309	7,06,479	26,27,972	17,91,812	8,36,160
AGR	0.7182*	0.6811*	0.6451*	0.5814*	0.7808*	0.6817*
CGR (in per cent)	14.12	15.98	12.08	17.67	18.59	15.98

* Significant at 5 per cent level. AGR – Annual Growth Rate. CGR – Compound Growth Rate.

The mean of interest received by societies at Nagercoil was increasing from Rs. 6.09 lakh in 1994-95 to Rs. 17.27 lakh in 2003-2004 whereas the mean of interest paid was increasing from Rs. 2.91 lakh to Rs. 10.21 lakh during the same period. The mean of spread was increasing from Rs. 3.18 lakh in 1994-1995 to Rs. 9.61 lakh in 2002-2003 and then it declined to Rs. 7.06 lakh in 2003-2004. The compound growth rates of interest received, interest paid and spread were 14.12, 15.98 and 12.08 respectively.

In the case of societies at Thuckalay, the mean of interest received was increasing from Rs.5.04 lakh in 1994-1995 to Rs. 26.27 lakh in 2003-2004 whereas the mean interest paid was increasing from Rs. 2.80 lakh to Rs. 17.92 lakh during the same period. The mean of spread was increasing from Rs. 2.24 lakh to Rs. 8.36 lakh during the period of the study. The compound growth rates of the spreads of the societies were 18.08 and 15.98 per cent respectively. The compound growth rates of interest received, interest paid and spread were 17.67, 18.59 and 15.98 respectively.

Investment Pattern of the Societies

The investments of the societies will bring income to the society and it is treated as other income which is discussed later on in this chapter. Proper investments are very essential for the successful performance of the societies. The societies invest their funds in the shares and other government securities. In the present study, the investments made by the societies are classified into share investments and other investments. The mean values of share and other investments from 1994-1995 to 2003-2004 of societies at Nagercoil and Thuckalay have been calculated and shown in Table 3.4.

The average share investments of the societies at Nagercoil was increasing from Rs. 1.18 lakh in 1994-95 to Rs. 2.97 lakh in 2003-04 whereas the average of other investments of the societies was increasing from Rs. 0.48 lakh to Rs. 3.10 lakh during the same period. The compound growth rates of share investments and other investments of the societies during the study period were 10.81 and 19.03 per cent respectively.

Table 3.4

Mean Values of Share Investments and other Investments of the Societies

Year	*Societies at Nagercoil*		*Societies at Thuckalay*	
	Share Investments (Rs.)	*Other Investments (Rs.)*	*Share Investments (Rs.)*	*Other Investments (Rs.)*
1994-95	1,18,440	48,070	1,26,877	26,115
1995-96	1,19,324	1,11,912	2,01,446	40,530
1996-97	1,29,144	1,03,339	3,10,077	62,342
1997-98	1,16,351	1,32,866	3,76,598	79,673
1998-99	1,27,913	1,69,050	4,35,296	1,14,931
1999-00	1,56,636	1,95,008	3,76,500	1,84,526
2000-01	1,77,049	2,19,539	5,01,719	2,33,650
2001-02	2,07,597	2,43,680	6,08,615	4,25,515
2002-03	2,36,984	2,64,337	6,15,992	4,50,659
2003-04	2,97,603	3,10,671	7,55,512	7,65,706
AGR	0.9081*	0.9904*	0.9763*	0.9094*
CGR (in percentage)	10.81	19.03	18.47	44.35

* Significant at 5 per cent level.
AGR – Annual Growth Rate.
CGR – Compound Growth Rate.

The mean of share investments of the societies at Thuckalay was from Rs. 1.27 lakh in 1994-95 to Rs. 7.55 lakh whereas the mean of other investments was increasing from Rs. 0.26 lakh to Rs. 7.66 lakh during the same period. The compound growth rate of the share investment and other investments in the Thuckalay societies were 18.47 and 44.35 per cent respectively.

The compound growth rate of other investments was greater than the compound growth rate of share investment in case of the societies at Nagercoil and Thuckalay. It indicates that the societies have more amount in other investments.

Bank Loans and Non Statutory Reserve

The societies borrow loans from the Kanyakumari District Central Co-operative Bank. The loan amount borrowed from the bank depends upon the need of the societies. The societies are also keeping some non statutory reserves. The mean values of bank loans and non statutory reserve of the societies from 1994-95 to 2003-04 have been calculated and shown in Table 3.5.

Table 3.5

Mean Values of Bank Loans and Non Statutory Reserve

Year	*Societies at Nagercoil*		*Societies at Thuckalay*	
	KDCC Bank Loan (Rs.)	*Non Statutory Reserve (Rs.)*	*KDCC Bank Loan (Rs.)*	*Non Statutory Reserve (Rs.)*
1994-95	3,39,681	1,56,977	16,46,768	19,584
1995-96	4,91,793	2,05,341	22,10,950	77,824
1996-97	7,25,239	2,30,074	40,89,567	78,862
1997-98	9,14,797	2,67,803	43,26,173	1,39,445
1998-99	12,84,332	3,02,286	39,56,350	2,01,730
1999-00	16,76,222	4,08,276	44,57,797	2,13,344
2000-01	16,65,892	5,00,348	45,00,401	6,02,412
2001-02	17,77,372	5,58,758	60,74,432	8,24,110
2002-03	19,60,006	6,47,059	70,85,293	9,54,363
2003-04	27,73,708	6,13,905	94,43,880	3,44,517
AGR	0.9745*	0.9802*	0.9283*	0.7828*
CGR (in percentage)	23.72	17.72	17.13	43.45

* Significant at 5 per cent level.

AGR – Annual Growth Rate.

CGR – Compound Growth Rate.

The average loan amount borrowed by societies at Nagercoil from the Kanyakumari District Central Cooperative Bank was increasing from Rs. 3.39 lakh in 1994-95 to Rs. 27.74 lakh in 2003-04. The average of non-statutory reserve of the societies was increasing from Rs. 1.57 lakh to 6.14 lakh during the same period. The compound growth rates of the above said indicators of the societies at Nagercoil were 23.72 and 17.72 per cent respectively.

In case of the societies at Thuckalay, the mean of loan amount borrowed from the bank was increasing from Rs. 16.47 lakh in 1994-95 to Rs. 94.44 lakh in 2003-04 and the average non-statutory reserve was increasing from Rs. 0.19 lakh to Rs. 3.44 lakh in 2003-04. The compound growth rates of loan borrowed from Kanyakumari District Central Cooperative Bank and non-statutory reserve were 17.13 and 43.45 per cent respectively.

Assets Quality in the Societies

The assets quality in the societies indicates the performance of the assets owned by the societies. It exhibits the nature of loans disbursed by the societies. By nature, the good loans are the loans which are generating interest income to the societies whereas the doubtful loans increase the Non-Performing Assets (NPAs) of the societies. The increase in NPAs delineates the profitability of the societies and creates the financial problems in the societies. Hence, an attempt is made to calculate the good and doubtful loans disbursed by the societies from 1994-95 to 2003-04. The mean values of good and doubtful loans disbursed by the societies are presented in Table 3.6.

The mean of good loans of the societies at Nagercoil was increasing from Rs. 49.22 lakh in 1994-95 to Rs. 172.08 lakh in 2003-04 whereas the mean of doubtful debts of the societies was increasing from Rs. 0.63 lakh to Rs. 3.21 lakh during the same period. The compound growth rates of good loans and doubtful loans in the societies at Nagercoil were 15.09 and 20.76 per cent respectively.

In Thuckalay, the mean of good loans of the societies was increasing from Rs. 32.18 lakh in 1994-95 to Rs. 151.74 lakh in 2003-04 whereas the mean of doubtful loans was increasing from Rs. 1.11 lakh to Rs. 11.82 lakh during the same period. The percentage of doubtful loans to total loan amounts during 1994-95 was 3.34 per cent whereas in 2003-04, it was 7.23 per cent. The compound growth rates of good loans and doubtful loans during the study period were 18.15 and 47.90 per cent respectively. It indicates that the growth of NPAs of societies at Thuckalay was growing faster than that of societies at Nagercoil.

Table 3.6

Means of Loans (Good) and Doubtful Loans

Year	*Societies at Nagercoil*		*Societies at Thuckalay*	
	Loans (Good) (Rs.)	*Loans (Doubtful) (Rs.)*	*Loans (Good) (Rs.)*	*Loans (Doubtful) (Rs.)*
1994-95	49,21,769	63,161	32,18,487	111,268
1995-96	57,06,869	72,591	43,21,227	128,038
1996-97	66,85,111	67,815	69,01,334	151,004
1997-98	77,61,875	1,15,684	73,73,836	4,52,728
1998-99	91,00,478	1,47,798	71,05,756	1,07,074
1999-00	108,89,843	1,00,804	103,01,836	2,04,068
2000-01	125,36,259	1,28,934	119,58,070	6,95,341
2001-02	140,04,864	2,63,231	141,11,695	7,02,499
2002-03	146,57,213	2,92,712	138,84,093	5,86,919
2003-04	172,08,060	3,21,267	151.74,152	11,81,820
AGR	0.9935*	0.9057*	0.9823*	0.8694*
CGR (in per cent)	15.09	20.76	18.15	47.9

* Significant at 5 per cent level.

AGR – Annual Growth Rate.

CGR – Compound Growth Rate.

Income and Expenditure of the Societies

The inflow of income to the societies is interest received and other incomes from various investments made by the societies. Similarly, the outflow of money is caused by the expenditures and also interest paid to the lenders. Since the interest received and paid have been discussed in the spread analysis, the present analysis covers only other incomes and establishment and contingent expenditures of the societies. In order to get a bird's view on the above aspects, the mean of other incomes and establishment and contingent expenditures have been calculated. The resulted mean values of the above said two important financial facts are presented in Table 3.7.

Table 3.7

Mean Values of Other Incomes and Expenditures of the Societies

Year	*Societies at Nagercoil*		*Societies at Thuckalay*	
	Other Incomes (Rs.)	*Establishment and Contingency Expenses (Rs.)*	*Other Incomes (Rs.)*	*Establishment and Contingency Expenses (Rs.)*
1994-95	10,669	88,058	6,533	77,782
1995-96	13,132	99,403	10,921	120,598
1996-97	17,194	115,463	14,209	178,391
1997-98	18,775	1,38,107	15,911	2,00,598
1998-99	25,356	1,72,289	27,266	2,88,073
1999-00	23,870	2,01,468	29,650	3,01,313
2000-01	31,199	2,31,346	28,602	3,23,385
2001-02	29,611	2,50,215	38,072	3,37,683
2002-03	23,659	2,57,550	27,871	2,57,210
2003-04	24,063	2,81,588	50,518	3,53,843
AGR	0.9925*	0.9924*	0.9255*	0.8902*
CGR (in per cent)	14.75	12.43	21.21	15.38

* Significant at 5 per cent level.

AGR – Annual Growth Rate

CGR – Compound Growth Rate

The mean of other incomes of the societies at Nagercoil was increasing from Rs. 0.11 lakh in 1994-95 to Rs. 0.24 lakh in 2003-04 whereas the mean of establishment and contingency expenses was increasing from Rs. 0.88 lakh to Rs. 2.82 lakh in 2003-04. The compound growth rates of the above said two items of the societies were 14.75 and 12.43 per cent respectively. The mean of other incomes of the societies at Thuckalay was increasing from

Rs. 0.06 lakh to Rs. 0.51 lakh during the period of the study. The mean of establishment and contingency expenses was increasing from Rs. 0.78 lakh in 1994-95 to Rs. 3.53 lakh in 2003-04. The compound growth rates of the above said two variables during the period of the study were 21.21 and 15.38 per cent respectively.

Interest Due and Overdue of the Societies

The interest due and overdues of the societies indicate income due to the societies. More amount of interest due and overdue will affect the circulation of fund and the profit of the society. It also indicates the inefficiency of the society in collecting the due amounts. The mean values of the interest due and interest overdue have been calculated to exhibit the trend of interest due and overdue. The resulted mean values of interest due and overdue with their annual growth rates and compound growth rates are shown in Table 3.8.

Table 3.8

Mean Values of Interest Due and Overdue

Year	*Societies at Nagercoil*		*Societies at Thuckalay*	
	Interest Due (Rs.)	*Interest Overdue (Rs.)*	*Interest Due (Rs.)*	*Interest Overdue (Rs.)*
1994-95	2,18,967	45,676	1,16,001	54,006
1995-96	2,71,097	57,842	2,11,173	57,745
1996-97	3,15,167	85,646	3,34,071	1,31,918
1997-98	3,38,830	1,38,360	2,30,286	2,12,976
1998-99	3,62,903	1,63,025	2,03,898	1,18,367
1999-00	4,36,969	1,52,129	2,44,490	1,49,754
2000-01	5,20,254	1,83,915	4,47,112	4,03,324
2001-02	6,11,299	2,51,867	5,06,408	4,48,680
2002-03	6,70,026	2,70,773	3,80,269	4,92,056
2003-04	6,59,516	2,74,824	3,47,195	7,25,722
AGR	0.9829*	0.9814*	0.7272*	0.9176*
CGR (in per cent)	13.60	22.24	11.69	32.60

* Significant at 5 per cent level.
AGR – Annual Growth Rate.
CGR – Compound Growth Rate.

The mean of interest due of the societies at Nagercoil was increasing from Rs. 2.19 lakh in 1994-95 to Rs. 6.59 lakh in 2003-04 whereas the mean of interest overdue was increasing from Rs. 0.46 lakh to Rs. 2.75 lakh during the same period. The compound growth rates of the above two variables during the period of the study were 13.60 and 22.24 per cent respectively. In the case of the societies at Thuckalay, the mean of interest due was increasing from Rs. 1.16 lakh in 1994-95 to Rs. 3.47 lakh in 2003-04 whereas the mean of interest overdue was increasing from Rs. 0.54 lakh to Rs. 7.26 lakh during the same period. The compound growth rates of interest due and interest overdue in the societies at Thuckalay during the period of the study were 11.69 and 32.60 per cent respectively.

Profit and Undistributed Profit of the Societies

The profit of the societies indicates the net profit of the societies. Out of the profit, the society declares the dividend to the members. A part of profit is not distributed to the members but accumulated as undistributed profit in the societies. Utilisation of the undistributed profit in proper way will increase the credit worthiness of the societies. Amount of undistributed profit reveals the business position. Since the profit is the important factor reflecting the financial performance of the society, it is included in the present study. The mean of total profit and undistributed profit of the societies from 1994-95 to 2003-04 have been computed and shown in Table 3.9.

The mean of profit of societies at Nagercoil was increasing from Rs. 2.39 lakh in 1994-95 to Rs. 7.42 lakh in 2003-04, whereas the undistributed profit was increasing from Rs. 0.09 lakh to Rs. 0.54 lakh during the same period. The compound growth rates of total profit and undistributed profit were 15.53 and 15.60 per cent respectively. The mean of profit of the societies at Thuckalay was increasing from Rs. 1.03 lakh in 1994-95 to Rs. 3.70 lakh in 2003-04, whereas the mean of undistributed profit was increasing from Rs. 0.65 lakh to Rs. 10.38 lakh during the same period. The compound growth rates of profit and undistributed profit during the period of the study were 17.79 and 41.89 per cent respectively. The compound growth rate of the undistributed profit of the societies at Thuckalay was greater than the compound growth rate of undistributed profit of the societies at Nagercoil, whereas the compound growth rate of profit was more or less similar in case of societies at Nagercoil and Thuckalay.

Table 3.9

Mean Values of Total Profit and Undistributed Profit of the Societies

Year	*Societies at Nagercoil*		*Societies at Thuckalay*	
	Total Profit (Rs.)	*Undistributed Profit (Rs.)*	*Total Profit (Rs.)*	*Undistributed Profit (Rs.)*
1994-95	2,38,836	9,423	1,03,031	64,967
1995-96	2,48,703	22,192	94,982	66,841
1996-97	2,81,561	45,508	1,87,649	68,225
1997-98	3,15,826	23,714	2,08,685	1,40,146
1998-99	3,69,493	30,838	3,63,118	2,25,335
1999-00	5,13,176	30,163	4,12,948	3,73,266
2000-01	5,27,715	40,194	5,29,531	4,58,028
2001-02	5,83,091	53,227	6,76,486	4,75,463
2002-03	6,85,130	51,608	4,25,670	10,12,102
2003-04	7,41,770	53,750	3,69,784	10,37,741
AGR	0.9911*	0.8371*	0.8624*	0.9217*
CGR (in per cent)	15.53	15.60	17.79	41.89

* Significant at 5 per cent level.
AGR – Annual Growth Rate
CGR – Compound Growth Rate

Sundry Debtors and Creditors of the Societies

The mean values of sundry debtors and creditors of the societies have been calculated. The compound growth rates of the sundry debtors and creditors have also been computed to exhibit the trend of the sundry debtors and creditors of the societies from 1994-95 to 2003-04. The resulted mean values of sundry debtors, sundry creditors and the respective compound growth rates are shown in Table 3.10.

Table 3.10

Mean Values of Sundry Debtors and Sundry Creditors of the Societies

Year	*Societies at Nagercoil*		*Societies at Thuckalay*	
	Sundry Debtors (Rs.)	*Sundry Creditors (Rs.)*	*Sundry Debtors (Rs.)*	*Sundry Creditors (Rs.)*
1994-95	76,595	47,938	68,049	2,722
1995-96	1,32,844	59,398	47,316	5,492
1996-97	1,16,812	71,380	2,30,414	11,796
1997-98	2,35,192	2,41,870	91,452	20,094
1998-99	3,06,010	3,23,817	1,13,178	16,590
1999-00	6,36,138	2,85,946	2,02,704	24,863
2000-01	6,62,070	3,15,675	3,49,974	20,225
2001-02	9,13,258	3,89,041	3,11,938	35,770
2002-03	5,71,163	4,35,839	3,69,162	29,945
2003-04	6,25,753	4,48,686	3,76,378	26,469
AGR	0.8632*	0.9579*	0.8863*	0.8949*
CGR (in per cent)	29.95	29.95	24.30	26.14

* Significant at 5 per cent level.

AGR – Annual Growth Rate.

CGR – Compound Growth Rate.

The mean of sundry debtors of the societies at Nagercoil was increasing from Rs. 0.77 lakh in 1994-95 to Rs. 6.26 lakh in 2003-04 whereas the mean of sundry creditors was increasing from Rs. 0.48 lakh to Rs. 4.49 lakh in 2003-04. The compound growth rates of the sundry debtors and sundry creditors of the societies in Nagercoil were 29.95 and 29.95 per cent respectively. In Thuckalay, the mean of sundry debtors of the societies was increasing from Rs. 0.68 lakh to Rs. 3.76 lakh during the same period. The mean of sundry creditors was increasing from Rs. 0.03 lakh in 1994-95 to Rs. 0.26 lakh in 2003-04. The compound growth rates of the above two financial indicators were 24.30 and

26.14 per cent respectively. The mean values of sundry debtors and creditors were comparatively higher in societies at Nagercoil than those at Thuckalay.

Cash in Hand and at Bank of the Societies

The most liquid assets of the financial organisations are cash in hand and cash at bank. The liquidity of the financial organisation is equally important along with the profitability of the organisation. In the present study, an analysis has been made to calculate the mean values of cash in hand and at bank of the societies at Nagercoil and Thuckalay from 1994-95 to 2003-04. The calculated mean values of cash in hand and at bank in the societies from 1994-95 to 2003-04 are shown in Table 3.11.

Table 3.11

Mean Values of Cash in Hand and Bank of the Societies

(Amount in Rs.)

Year	*Societies at Nagercoil*		*Societies at Thuckalay*	
	Cash in Hand	*Cash at Bank*	*Cash in Hand*	*Cash at Bank*
1994-95	1,768	2,04,678	12,595	36,650
1995-96	4,652	90,927	6,088	60,584
1996-97	3,433	2,99,749	5,925	2,02,866
1997-98	4,256	1,81,003	14,815	62,920
1998-99	2,323	2,47,887	5,327	1,23,548
1999-00	5,016	1,45,348	14,891	87,078
2000-01	7,686	1,25,886	17,080	1,40,106
2001-02	6,749	1,26,306	22,353	1,04,865
2002-03	7,783	2,04,671	17,842	60,147
2003-04	6,794	68,205	8,484	1,06,675
AGR	0.8219*	-0.4001	0.4499	0.1248
CGR (in per cent)	14.02	-5.97	7.59	5.17

* Significant at 5 per cent level.

AGR – Annual Growth Rate

CGR – Compound Growth Rate

The mean of cash in hand of the societies at Nagercoil was increasing from Rs. 0.02 lakh in 1994-95 to Rs. 0.07 lakh in 2003-04 whereas the mean of cash at bank was decreasing from Rs. 2.05 lakh to Rs. 0.68 lakh during the same period. The compound growth rates of cash in hand and cash at bank were 14.02 per cent and –5.97 per cent respectively. It reveals that the cash at bank per society was gradually declining over the study period. In Thuckalay, the mean of cash in hand was declining from Rs. 0.13 lakh in 1994-95 to Rs. 0.08 lakh in 2003-04 whereas the mean of cash at bank is increasing from Rs. 0.37 lakh in 1994-95 to Rs. 1.07 lakh in 2003-04. The compound growth rates of cash in hand and at bank were 7.59 and 5.17 per cent respectively. The increase in cash in hand and at bank in the societies at Thuckalay were insignificant.

Furniture of the Societies

The fixed assets owned by the societies are the furniture and fittings. The investment on furniture and fittings in the societies have been examined with the help of mean of the values of furniture of the societies at Nagercoil and Thuckalay from 1994-95 to 2003-04. The mean values of amount invested in furniture and the compound growth rate of value of furniture are shown in Table 3.12.

The mean of furniture value of the societies was increasing from Rs. 0.11 lakh in 1994-95 to Rs. 0.18 lakh in 2003-04. The compound growth rate of the furniture value was only 5.95 per cent in societies at Nagercoil during the period of the study. In societies at Thuckalay, the mean of furniture value of the societies was increasing from Rs. 0.12 lakh in 1994-95 to Rs. 0.40 lakh in 2003-04. The compound growth rate of furniture value of the societies at Thuckalay during the period of the study was 14.08 per cent.

Table 3.12

Mean Values of Furniture of the Societies

(Amount in Rs.)

Year	*Societies at Nagercoil*	*Societies at Thuckalay*
1994-95	11,418	12,330
1995-96	11,824	16,010
1996-97	13,706	22,672
1997-98	15,011	28,326
1998-99	15,833	27,262
1999-00	18,034	37,466
2000-01	18,282	43,802
2001-02	18,662	43,858
2002-03	18,773	38,528
2003-04	17,872	40,322
AGR	0.9292*	0.9175*
CGR (in per cent)	5.95	14.08

* Significant at 5 per cent level.

AGR – Annual Growth Rate.

CGR – Compound Growth Rate.

ECONOMIC VIABILITY OF THE SOCIETIES

The economic viability of the society represents the viability of the society to carry on its functions. In general, the economic viability of the financial organisation is evaluated with the help of its demand, collection, overdues and the per cent of overdues to demand.[1] The higher percentage of overdues to demand in the financial organisation indicates the financial non viability of the organisation. In the present study, the same analysis has been used to analyse the financial viability of the cooperative societies at Nagercoil and Thuckalay.

Economic Viability of the Societies at Nagercoil

The mean values of demand, collection, overdues and the percentage of overdues to demand of the societies at Nagercoil have been computed and shown in Table 3.13.

Table 3.13

Economic Viability of the Societies at Nagercoil

(Amount in Rs.)

Year	*Mean of Demand for Loans*	*Mean of Collection of Loans*	*Mean of Overdues*	*Overdues to demand (in percentage)*
1994-95	39,24,702	24,18,415	15,06,287	38.38
1995-96	39,12,401	23,95,070	15,17,331	38.78
1996-97	45,50,322	29,16,388	16,33,934	35.91
1997-98	55,22,093	38,27,985	16,94,108	30.68
1998-99	64,56,811	47,30,718	17,26,093	26.73
1999-00	74,99,590	56,66,579	18,33,011	24.44
2000-01	81,43,041	62,21,633	19,21,408	23.59
2001-02	85,16,153	65,14,926	20,01,227	23.49
2002-03	93,17,040	71,23,732	21,93,308	23.54
2003-04	104,51,155	81,49,124	23,02,031	22.03

The mean of demand for loans of the societies at Nagercoil was increasing from Rs. 39.25 lakh in 1994-95 to Rs. 104.51 lakh in 2003-04 whereas the collection per society was also increasing from Rs. 24.18 lakh to Rs. 81.49 lakh in 2003-04. The overdues per society was increasing from Rs. 15.06 to Rs. 23.02 lakh during the same period. The percentage of overdues to demand per society was declining from 38.38 per cent to 22.03 per cent. The percentage of overdues to demand in the societies is comparatively less than the percentage of overdues to demand in the cooperative banks because the loans disbursed by the societies are attached with the source deduction for the repayment of loan.

To ascertain the economic viability the societies at Nagercoil were classified on the basis of the percentage of overdues to demand. The mean of percentage of overdues to demand for 10 years per society was computed for the classification of economic viability of the societies. These were confined to less than 20 per cent, 20 to 30 per cent, 30 to 40 per cent, 40 to 50 per cent and above 50 per cent. The distribution of societies are shown in Table 3.14.

Table 3.14

Distribution of Societies in Nagercoil on the Basis of Economic Viability

Sl. No.	*Mean of Overdues to Demand Ratio*	*Number of Societies*	*Percentage to the total*
1.	Less than 20 per cent	5	21.74
2.	20-30 per cent	6	26.09
3.	31-40 per cent	4	17.39
4.	41-50 per cent	5	21.74
5.	Above 50 per cent	3	13.04
	Total	23	100.00

In total, nearly 48 percentage of the societies at Nagercoil have the economic viability since the respective overdue ratios to its demand are less than 30 per cent. The societies which have the overdue ratio of above 50 per cent constitute 13.04 percentage.

Economic Viability of the Societies at Thuckalay

The economic viability of the societies at Thuckalay was examined with the help of demand, collection, overdues and the percentage of overdues to demand from 1994-95 to 2003-04 of each society. The mean values of demand, collection, overdues and percentage of overdues to demand of the societies at Thuckalay from 1994-95 to 2003-04 have been calculated and presented in Table 3.15.

Table 3.15

Economic Viability of the Societies at Thuckalay

Year	*Mean of Demand (Rs.)*	*Mean of Collection (Rs.)*	*Mean of Overdues (Rs.)*	*Overdues to Demand (in percentage)*
1994-95	26,45,844	19,97,386	6,48,458	24.51
1995-96	34,73,266	26,75,200	7,98,066	22.98
1996-97	42,38,762	33,02,100	9,36,662	22.09
1997-98	55,21,780	43,94,506	11,27,274	25.65
1998-99	57,88,351	45,77,541	12,10,810	26.45
1999-00	78,06,230	61,62,457	16,43,773	26.67
2000-01	67,91,702	53,40,185	14,51,517	21.37
2001-02	88,08,524	68,07,041	20,01,483	29.54
2002-03	75,55,646	55,57,811	19,97,835	26.44
2003-04	115,32,407	86,31,045	28,01,362	24.29

The mean of demand of the societies was increasing from Rs. 26.46 lakh in 1994-95 to Rs. 115.32 lakh in 2003-04 whereas the mean of collection of the societies at Thuckalay was increasing from Rs. 19.97 lakh to Rs. 86.31 lakh in 2003-04. The mean of overdues was also increasing from Rs. 6.48 lakh to Rs. 28.01 lakh during the same period. The percentage of overdues to demand varied from 21.37 per cent to 29.54 per cent during the study period.

Since, the percentage of overdues to demand in the societies varies from one society to another, the present study has made an attempt to analyse the number of societies under different economic viability. For that the mean value of the percentage of overdues to demand for each society was calculated. The percentage of overdues to demand was confined to less than 20 per cent, 20 to 30 per cent, 31 to 40 per cent, 41 to 50 per cent and above 50 per cent. The distribution of societies at Thuckalay on the basis of mean of overdue ratios is exhibited in Table 3.16.

Table 3.16

Distribution of Societies at Thuckalay by Economic Viability

Sl. No.	*Mean of Overdues to Demand Ratio*	*Number of Societies*	*Percentage to Total*
1.	Less than 20 per cent	1	7.69
2.	20-30 per cent	5	38.46
3.	31 – 40 per cent	4	30.77
4.	41 – 50 per cent	2	15.39
5.	Above 50 per cent	1	7.69
	Total	13	100.00

Among the societies at Thuckalay, 38.46 percentage societies had 20 to 30 per cent overdue ratio and 30.77 percentage of the societies had 31 to 40 per cent overdue ratio. Only 7.69 percentage of the societies had above 50 per cent overdue ratio and the societies which had less than 20 per cent overdue ratio was also 7.69 percentage.

FINANCIAL PERFORMANCE OF THE SOCIETIES

Financial performance of the societies was analysed with the help of ratio analysis. Ratio analysis is a powerful device to analyse and interpret the financial health of the firm. This not only helps the management in decision making and control but also serves as an useful tool for all, concerned with the firm. The financial performance of the societies was evaluated in three different dimensions namely operational efficiency, financial efficiency and liquidity efficiency.

Operational Efficiency of the Societies

Operational efficiency refers to the most efficient use of resources, so as to generate optimum returns.

The operational efficiency of the society has been analysed with the help of the following ratios.

(i) Owned funds to Borrowed funds

(ii) Borrowed funds to Working capital

(iii) Credit to Deposits ratio and

(iv) Outstanding of loans to Working capital.

The ratio of owned funds to borrowed funds is calculated by the formula:

$$\frac{\text{Owned funds}}{\text{Borrowed funds}} \times 100$$

The ratio of borrowings to working capital indicates the proportion of borrowings to working capital and is worked out by the formula:

$$\frac{\text{Borrowings}}{\text{Working Capital}} \times 100$$

The ratio of Credit to Deposit is calculated by the formula:

$$\frac{\text{Credit}}{\text{Deposits}} \times 100$$

The ratio of outstanding loans to working capital measures the credit capacity of the society. This ratio is calculated by

$$\frac{\text{Outstanding Loan}}{\text{Working Capital}} \times 100$$

The standard deviation and the coefficient of variation of the four ratios have also been computed to analyse the consistency of the ratios during the study period. The computed operational efficiency ratios of the societies at Nagercoil and Thuckalay are exhibited in Table 3.17.

Table 3.17

Operational Efficiency of the Societies

(Ratios in per cent)

Sl. No.	*Operational Efficiency Ratios*	*Societies at Nagercoil*			*Societies at Thuckalay*		
		Mean	*Standard Deviation*	*Coefficient of Variation*	*Mean*	*Standard Deviation*	*Coefficient of Variation*
1.	Own funds to borrowed funds	46.83	8.52	18.19	72.3	15.3	21.16
2.	Borrowed funds to working capital	43.4	12.92	29.76	47.31	5.31	11.22
3.	Credit to deposit	134.58	13.04	9.69	294.90	64.75	21.96
4.	Outstanding loans to working capital	78.89	7.82	9.91	68.51	9.37	13.68

From Table 3.17, it can be observed that the mean of own funds to borrowed funds of the societies at Nagercoil was 46.83 percentage whereas the coefficient of variation was 18.19 percentage. In the societies at Thuckalay, the mean and co-efficient of variation of the ratios were 72.3 and 21.16 percentage respectively. The high ratio represents the corresponding increase in own funds.

It is clear that the share of borrowings to working capital of societies at Nagercoil was 43.4 per cent since its mean value was 43.4 whereas its coefficient of variation was 29.76 per cent. In the case of societies at Thuckalay, this mean ratio was 47.31 and its coefficient of variation was 11.22 per cent. The analysis reveals that the dependence on borrowings for their working capital in societies was around 45 per cent. That means the societies depend more on deposits, share capital and reserves for their working capital but the dependence was not too high.

The mean of credit to deposit ratio of the societies at Nagercoil was 134.58 with the coefficient of variation of 9.69 percentage. In the case of societies at Thuckalay, the mean and coefficient of variation were 294.9 and 21.96 per cent respectively. It reveals that the society's efficiency in credit generation was higher whereas it was very high in case of societies at Thuckalay.

The trend in the bank's credit granting capacity is reflected by its ratio of outstanding loans to working capital. The mean of these ratios of the societies at Nagercoil was 78.89 whereas its coefficient of variation was 9.91 per cent. In the case of societies at Thuckalay, the mean and coefficient of variation of these ratios were 68.51 and 13.68 per cent respectively. It reveals that the working capital of the societies was more than the outstanding loans of the societies. It shows that the society's performance in deploying funds was not satisfactory.

Financial Efficiency of the Societies

The financial efficiency of the societies was examined with the help of the profitability ratios of the societies. These ratios are:

(*i*) Total expenses to Total income;

(*ii*) Net profit to Working capital;

(*iii*) Interest paid to Interest received; and

(*iv*) Non-interest expenses to Non-interest income.

The ratio of total expenses to total income is calculated by:

$$\frac{\text{Total Expenditure}}{\text{Total Income}} \times 100$$

The net profit to working capital ratio represents the bank's efficiency in making higher returns out of the working capital. The net profit should be enough to provide optimum returns on the working capital. This ratio is calculated by the formula:

$$\frac{\text{Net Profit}}{\text{Working Capital}} \times 100$$

The interest paid to interest received ratio has been worked out by the formula:

$$\frac{\text{Interest Paid}}{\text{Interest received}} \times 100$$

The non-interest expense to non-interest income ratio is worked out to find out the bank's expenses and income other than the interest paid and interest received. The formula used for this ratio is

$$\frac{\text{Non - interest Expenses}}{\text{Non - interest Income}} \times 100$$

In the present study, the mean of the above said four ratios in the societies at Nagercoil and Thuckalay have been computed from the respective ratios from 1994-95 to 2003-04. The standard deviation and the coefficient of variation of these ratios have also been calculated to reveal the consistency of the ratios during the period of the study. The computed ratios are displayed in Table 3.18.

Table 3.18 shows that the mean of ratios between total expenses to total income of the societies at Nagercoil was 59.08

Table 3.18

Financial Efficiency of the Societies

(Ratios in percentage)

Sl. No.	Profitability Ratios	Societies at Nagercoil			Societies at Thuckalay		
		Mean	Standard Deviation	Coefficient of Variation	Mean	Standard Deviation	Coefficient of Variation
1.	Total expenses to Total income	59.08	15.63	26.46	76.1	4.84	6.36
2.	Net profit to Working capital	4.77	0.35	7.34	3.25	1.04	0.32
3.	Interest paid to Interest received	46.99	1.25	26.60	62.30	6.11	9.81
4.	Non-interest expenses to Non-interest income	835.83	167.52	20.04	1052.46	176.95	16.81

whereas the coefficient of variation was 26.46 per cent. In the societies at Thuckalay, the mean and coefficient of variation of these ratios were 76.1 and 6.36 per cent respectively. This ratio was comparatively less in the societies at Nagercoil because of the profitability of the societies. The higher ratios of total expenses to total income may be caused by a few loss making societies at Thuckalay. Apart from that the high ratio means that the total expense is increasing at a rate higher than that of the total income.

It was found that the net profit to working capital ratio was higher in the societies at Nagercoil, since the respective mean of this ratio was 4.77 whereas the coefficient of variation was 7.34 per cent. In the case of the societies at Thuckalay, the mean and coefficient of variation of this ratio were 3.25 and 0.32 per cent respectively. The low ratio is caused by a few loss making societies.

The mean and coefficient of variation of the ratios of interest paid to interest received of the societies at Nagercoil were 46.99 and 26.60 per cent respectively. In the case of the societies at Thuckalay these two were 62.3 and 9.81 per cent respectively. The higher ratio results in a gradual fall in profitability of the societies.

The mean of the ratios of non-interest expenses to non-interest income of the societies at Nagercoil was 835.83 per cent whereas in the societies at Thuckalay, it was 1052.46 per cent. The coefficient of variation of these ratios of the societies at Nagercoil and Thuckalay were 20.04 and 16.81 per cent respectively. The non-interest expenses of the societies were very high compared to non-interest income thus bringing down the profit margin.

Liquidity Efficiency of the Societies

The liquidity efficiency of the societies is analysed with the help of three ratios:

(i) Cash in hand and at bank to Borrowed funds;

(ii) Investment to Deposits; and

(iii) Spread to Total assets.

Cash is kept with the society to meet the demands of the depositors. Higher the cash maintained in the bank higher will be the liquidity and *vice versa*. And higher the cash maintained in the bank less will be the profitability and vice-versa. The following formula is used for calculating the ratio:

$$\frac{\text{Cash in Hand and at Bank}}{\text{Borrowed Funds}} \times 100$$

Investment to deposits indicates the relationship between investment made by the societies and the deposits received by the societies. The formula used to study the relationship is

$$\frac{\text{Investment}}{\text{Deposits}} \times 100$$

The ratio of spread to total assets indicates the contribution of operating income in the total assets. It is calculated by

$$\frac{\text{Spread}}{\text{Total Assets}} \times 100$$

The higher ratio indicates the higher contribution of spread in total assets.

In the present study, the mean of the above said four ratios, standard deviation and coefficient of variation of the societies at Nagercoil and Thuckalay have been computed separately and shown in Table 3.19.

The mean of the ratios of cash in hand and at bank to borrowed funds of societies at Nagercoil was 19.98 per cent with the coefficient of variation of 90.54 per cent. In the case of the societies at Thuckalay, the mean and coefficient of variation of the ratios were 12.64 per cent and 30.76 per cent. The mean of investment to deposits in Societies at Nagercoil was 0.07 per cent whereas in the societies at Thuckalay, it was 0.27 per cent. The mean of the ratios of spread to total assets of societies at Nagercoil was 31.08 per cent with the coefficient of variation of 27.12 per cent. In the societies at Thuckalay, the mean and coefficient of variation of the ratios were 34.27 and 26.93 per cent respectively. By that, the analysis infers that the liquidity of the societies is not up to the mark.

Table 3.19

Liquidity Efficiency of the Societies

(Ratios in per cent)

Sl. No.	Ratios	Societies at Nagercoil			Societies at Thuckalay		
		Mean	Standard Deviation	Coefficient of Variation	Mean	Standard Deviation	Coefficient of Variation
1.	Cash in hand and at bank to Borrowed funds	19.98	18.09	90.54	12.64	3.89	30.76
2.	Investments to Deposits	0.07	0.01	14.29	0.27	0.05	18.52
3.	Spread to Total assets	31.08	8.43	27.12	34.27	9.23	26.93

DETERMINANTS OF PROFIT OF THE EMPLOYEES COOPERATIVE THRIFT AND CREDIT SOCIETIES

The Employee Cooperative Thrift and Credit Societies perform a vital role in the enrichment of the employees' standard of living. While their functioning is essential for the credit flow to employees, their existence should be justified by their operational results. In other words, unless they earn profits continuously, their functioning will be difficult and they might fall sick. So the determinants of profits should be identified.

Even though, there are so many determinants of profit in the societies, the present study confine these determinants to reserve fund, deposits, borrowings, advances, investments, working capital, overdues and spread. The above said determinants are identified with the help of reviews of Thiruthuvadoss (2004).[2] The above said eight variables are included as independent variables whereas the net profit is taken as the dependent variable. The multiple regression analysis has been administered to analyse the impact of independent variables on the net profit of the societies.

The fitted regression model is

$$y = a+b_1x_1+b_2x_2+b_3x_3+b_4bx_4+b_5x_5+b_6x_6+b_7x_7+b_8x_8+e$$

Whereas y - Net profit of the societies

x_1 - Reserve fund of the societies

x_2 - Deposits of the societies

x_3 - Borrowings of the societies

x_4 - Advances of the societies

x_5 - Investments of the societies

x_6 - Working capital of the societies

x_7 - Overdues of the societies

x_8 - Spread of the societies

$b_1, b_2 - b_8$ - Regression coefficients of independent variables

e - error term and

a - constant

Determinants

The data related to the above said variables of the societies at Nagercoil, from 1994-95 to 2003-04 were used to find out the impact of independent variables on net profit. The resulted regression coefficients of the independent variables are shown in Table 3.20.

Table 3.20

Determinants of Profit of the Societies at Nagercoil

Sl. No.	*Independent Variables*	*Regression Coefficient*	*Standard Error*	*'t'-Statistics*	*P-Value*
1.	Reserve Fund	-.4113	.1117	-3.6822*	0.01429
2.	Deposits	0.0172	.0624	0.2756	0.4473
3.	Borrowings	0.0796	.1133	0.7026	0.2919
4.	Advances	-0.0572	.0914	-0.6258	0.3303
5.	Investments	0.0693	.1242	0.5579	0.3917
6.	Working Capital	-0.2319	.0731	-3.1724*	0.01943
7.	Overdues	-0.5236	.1409	-3.7161*	0.01221
8.	Spread	0.7317	.1324	5.5264*	0.0000
	Constant	-2.0933			
	R^2	0.8193			
	F-Statistics	8.9432*			

* Significant at 5 per cent level.

The significantly influencing independent variables on the net profit of the societies were reserve fund, working capital, overdues and spread. A unit increase in spread will result in an increase in net profit of the societies by 0.7317 units. A unit increase in reserve fund, working capital and overdues result in a decrease in net profit of the societies by 0.4113, 0.2319 and 0.5236 units respectively. The changes in included independent variables explain the changes in net profit of the societies at Nagercoil to the extent of 81.93 per cent. The significant 'F' statistics reveals the viability of the fitted regression model.

Determinants of Net Profit of the Societies at Thuckalay

The impact of selected eight independent variables on the net profit of the societies at Thuckalay has been examined with the help of multiple regression analysis. The data related to the above said eight independent variables and the respective net profit from 1994-95 to 2003-04 are taken for analysis. The same regression model is fitted.

$$y = a+b_1x_1+b_2x_2+b_3x_3+b_4bx_4+b_5x_5+b_6x_6+b_7x_7+b_8x_8+e$$

Whereas y - Net profit of the societies

x_1 - Reserve fund of the societies

x_2 - Deposits of the societies

x_3 - Borrowings of the societies

x_4 - Advances of the societies

x_5 - Investments of the societies

x_6 - Working capital of the societies

x_7 - Overdues of the societies

x_8 - Spread of the societies

$b_1, b_2 - b_8$ - Regression coefficients of independent variables

a - constant and

a - error term.

The significantly influencing independent variables on net profit of the societies at Thuckalay were reserve fund, advances, working capital, overdues and spread. A unit increase in spread and advances results in an increase in net profit of the societies by 0.5134 and 0.1673 units respectively. At the same time a unit increase in reserve fund, working capital and overdues results in a decline in net profit of the societies by 0.3029, 0.1708 and 0.3091 units respectively. The change in included independent variables explains the change in net profit to the extent of 86.43 per cent.

The resulted regression coefficients of independent variables are presented in Table 3.21.

Table 3.21

Determinants of Profit of Societies at Thuckalay

Sl. No.	*Independent Variables*	*Regression Coefficient*	*Standard Error*	*'t'-Statistics*	*P-Value*
1.	Reserve Fund	-.3029	.0993	-3.0504*	0.0034
2.	Deposits	0.0534	.0362	1.4751	0.0919
3.	Borrowings	0.0941	.1108	0.8493	0.3108
4.	Advances	0.1673	.0504	3.3194*	0.0011
5.	Investments	0.0521	.1371	0.3801	0.5309
6.	Working Capital	-0.1708	.0409	-4.1863*	0.0039
7.	Overdues	-0.3091	.0817	-3.7834*	0.0017
8.	Spread	0.5134	.1108	4.6336*	0.0000
	Constant	-3.1143			
	R^2	0.8643			
	F-Statistics	9.0317*			

* Significant at 5 per cent level.

SUMMARY

The financial analysis reveals that share capital, deposits, profit and loan disbursed were increasing during the study period, whereas the number of members was decreasing. The decrease in number of members will certainly affect the survival of the societies. So in the next chapter the profile of the members, their attitude towards the society and the association between their profile and attitude are analysed.

REFERENCES

1. Devaraj, T.S., "An Analysis of Working of District Cooperative Central Bank, Hassan Karnataka", *The Maharashtra Cooperative Quarterly*, 83(2), October-December, 1999, pp. 49-56.

2. Thiruthuvadoss, S.P., "Determinants of Profit in District Central Cooperative Banks", *Tamil Nadu Journal of Cooperation*, 4(5), March 2004, pp. 11-14.

4

PROFILE OF THE MEMBERS AND THEIR ATTITUDE TOWARDS THE ECTCS

INTRODUCTION

The members are the pillars of the ECTCS They expect some services from the societies. If they are satisfied with the services offered by the societies, the societies can attract more members. It is highly essential for the growth of the societies. The societies provide two important services namely accepting the deposits and providing loans to their members. The members perceive that the services offered by the societies are more important than anything else. Hence, the present study has made an attempt to analyse the members' view on the various services offered by the societies.

PROFILE OF THE MEMBERS

Since the attitude and problem perception among the members are highly related with the profile of the members, the profile of the members is also focussed in the study. Even though the profile of the members are too many, the present study confines these profile variables to gender, age, level of education, occupation, subsidiary occupation, marital status, family size, personal income, personality traits, family income, monthly expenditure and monthly savings.

Gender of the Members

The gender of the members may have its own influence on the attitude formation, problem perception, repayment, behaviour and knowledge regarding the societies. So it is included as one of the profile variables. The members belonging to the societies are both males and females. The gender of the members selected for the present study is illustrated in Table 4.1.

Table 4.1

Gender of the Members

Sl. No.	*Gender*	*Societies at Nagercoil*		*Societies at Thuckalay*		*Total*	
		No. of Members	*Percent-age*	*No. of Members*	*Percent-age*	*No. of Members*	*Percent-age*
1.	Males	262	84.52	219	86.22	481	85.28
2.	Females	48	15.48	35	13.78	83	14.72
	Total	310	100.00	254	100.00	564	100.00

Source: Primary Data.

In total, the male members in the present study constitute 85.28 per cent. In the societies at Nagercoil, the male members constitute 84.52 per cent, whereas in the societies at Thuckalay, the male members constitute 86.22 per cent to the total. The analysis infers that the male members are dominating in the societies at Nagercoil and Thuckalay.

Age of the Members

Since the age of the members may indicate their level of exposure, experience and maturity, it is included as one of the profile variables in the present study. In general, the aged members may have better knowledge, exposure and experience compared to the youngsters. In the present study, the age of the members was confined to less than 30 years, 30 to 35, 36 to 40, 41 to 45, 46 to 50, 51 to 55 and above 55 years. The distribution of members on the basis of their age is shown in Table 4.2.

Table 4.2

Age of the Members

Sl. No.	*Age*	*Societies at Nagercoil*		*Societies at Thuckalay*		*Total*	
		No. of Members	*Percent-age*	*No. of Members*	*Percent-age*	*No. of Members*	*Percent-age*
1.	Less than 30	25	8.06	7	2.76	32	5.67
2.	30 – 35	31	10.00	19	7.48	50	8.87
3.	36 – 40	55	17.74	48	18.90	103	18.26
4.	41 – 45	62	20.00	58	22.83	120	21.27
5.	46 – 50	53	17.10	56	22.05	109	19.33
6.	51 – 55	43	13.87	44	17.32	87	15.43
7.	Above 55	41	13.23	22	8.66	63	11.17
	Total	310	100.00	254	100.00	564	100.00

Source: Primary Data.

The common age groups among the members are 41 to 45, 46 to 50 and 36 to 40 years which constitute 21.27, 19.33 and 18.26 per cent to the total respectively. Members who were at the age of less than 30 years constitute only 5.67 per cent to the total. In societies at Nagercoil, the first two common age groups were 41 to 45 and 36 to 40 years which constitute 20.00 and 17.74 per cent to the total respectively. In societies at Thuckalay, the majority age groups were 41 to 45 years and 46 to 50 years which constitute 22.83 and 22.05 per cent to the total respectively.

Level of Education of the Members

The education of the members may represent their level of understanding, expectations and perceptions on the various services offered by the societies. So the level of education is included as one of the profile variables. The level of education was confined to school level, graduation, post-graduation, professional and others. The distribution of members on the basis of their level of education is exhibited in Table 4.3.

Table 4.3

Level of Education of the Members

Sl. No.	Level of Education	Societies at Nagercoil		Societies at Thuckalay		Total	
		No. of Members	Percent-age	No. of Members	Percent-age	No. of Members	Percent-age
1.	School Level	69	22.26	53	20.87	122	21.63
2.	Graduation	113	36.45	94	37.01	207	36.70
3.	Post-graduation	89	28.71	65	25.59	154	27.30
4.	Professional	26	8.39	19	7.48	45	7.98
5.	Others	13	4.19	23	9.06	36	6.38
	Total	310	100.00	254	100.00	564	100.00

Source: Primary Data.

The most common levels of education among the members were graduation, post graduation and school level education which constitute 36.70, 27.30 and 21.63 per cent to the total respectively. The common levels of education of the members in societies at Nagercoil were graduation and post-graduation which constitute 36.45 and 28.71 per cent to the total respectively. In societies at Thuckalay, graduation and post-graduation members constitute 37.01 and 25.59 per cent to the total respectively. Members who have only school level education in societies at Nagercoil and Thuckalay constitute 22.26 and 20.87 per cent to its respective total.

Occupation of the Members

Since the occupation shows their level of earning and also their knowledge on the various activities of the societies, it is included as one of the profile variables. The members were classified into ordinary workers, technical workers, supervisors, clerical assistants, teachers and professionals in the present study. The number of members under different occupations is illustrated in Table 4.4.

Table 4.4

Occupation of the Members

Sl. No.	Occupation	Societies at Nagercoil		Societies at Thuckalay		Total	
		No. of Members	Percentage	No. of Members	Percentage	No. of Members	Percentage
1.	Ordinary workers	41	13.23	39	15.35	80	14.18
2.	Technical workers	5	1.61	6	2.36	11	1.95
3.	Supervisors	24	7.74	17	6.69	41	7.27
4.	Clerical Assistants	136	43.87	121	47.64	257	45.57
5.	Teachers	83	26.77	52	20.47	135	23.94
6.	Professionals	21	6.77	19	7.48	40	7.09
	Total	310	100.00	254	100.00	564	100.00

Source: Primary Data.

Most of the members were clerical assistants and teachers who constitute 45.57 and 23.94 per cent to the total respectively. The ordinary workers constitute 13.23 and 15.35 per cent to the respective total in societies at Nagercoil and Thuckalay. Clerical assistants and teachers constitute 70.65 and 68.11 per cent to the total of the societies at Nagercoil and Thuckalay.

Subsidiary Occupation

Subsidiary occupation indicates the occupation of the members apart from the main occupation. Since the subsidiary occupation provides extra income to the members, it may increase the potential for savings. It also has its own impact on the repayment behaviour among the members. Hence, it is included as one of the profile variables. In the present study, the subsidiary occupations were grouped into agriculture, private employment, business, finance and others. In total, 24.65 per cent of the members have their own subsidiary occupation. The distribution of members on the basis of their subsidiary occupation is shown in Table 4.5.

Table 4.5
Subsidiary Occupation of the Members

Sl. No.	*Subsidiary Occupation*	*Societies at Nagercoil*		*Societies at Thuckalay*		*Total*	
		No. of Members	*Percent-age*	*No. of Members*	*Percent-age*	*No. of Members*	*Percent-age*
1.	Agriculture	31	37.80	14	24.56	45	32.37
2.	Private Employment	17	20.73	11	19.30	28	20.14
3.	Business	13	15.85	12	21.05	25	17.99
4.	Finance	19	23.17	15	26.32	34	24.46
5.	Others	2	2.44	5	8.77	7	5.04
	Total	82	100.00	57	100.00	139	100.00

Source: Primary Data.

The important subsidiary occupations of the members were agriculture and finance which constitute 32.37 and 24.46 per cent to the total respectively. Members who had a subsidiary occupation of private employment and business constitute 20.14 and 17.99 per cent to the total respectively. In societies at Nagercoil, the first two important subsidiary occupations were agriculture and finance which constitute 37.80 and 23.17 per cent to the total respectively. In societies at Thuckalay, the first two subsidiary occupations were finance and agriculture which constitute 26.32 and 24.56 per cent to the total respectively.

Marital Status of the Members

The marital status of the members may have its own impact on income and expenditure. So the present study includes marital status and classified them into unmarried, married, separated and widows/widowers. The distribution of members on the basis of their marital status is shown in Table 4.6.

Table 4.6

Marital Status of the Members

Sl. No.	*Marital Status*	*Societies at Nagercoil*		*Societies at Thuckalay*		*Total*	
		No. of Members	*Percent-age*	*No. of Members*	*Percent-age*	*No. of Members*	*Percent-age*
1.	Unmarried	14	4.52	4	1.57	18	3.19
2.	Married	273	88.06	231	90.94	504	89.36
3.	Separated	15	4.84	9	3.54	24	4.26
4.	Widow/Widower	8	2.58	10	3.94	18	3.19
	Total	310	100.00	254	100.00	564	100.00

Source: Primary Data.

The most common marital status among the members in the present study was married. In societies at Nagercoil, married members constitute 88.06 per cent to the total whereas in the societies at Thuckalay, it constitutes 90.94 per cent to the total. The analysis shows that the main marital status among the members in the present study is married.

Family Size of the Members

The family size represents the number of members living together in a family. Since the family size has its own impact on the borrowing of loans and repayment behaviour among the members, it is included in the present study. In the present study, the family size of the members was confined to less than 3 members, 3 to 4, 5 to 6, 7 to 8 and above 8 members. The distribution of members on the basis of their family size is illustrated in Table 4.7.

The family sizes of the members of 5–6 and 3 to 4 members were 36.17 and 29.61 per cent to the total respectively. Members who had a family size of above 8 members constitute 10.11 per cent to the total. The common family sizes among the members of the societies at Nagercoil were 3 to 4 and 5 to 6 members which constitute 30.65 and 30.00 per cent to the respective total of 310 members whereas in the societies at Thuckalay, these two were 5 to 6 members and 3 to 4 members which constitute 43.70 and 28.35 per cent to its respective total of 254 respondents.

Table 4.7

Family Size of the Members

Sl. No.	*Family Size*	*Societies at Nagercoil*		*Societies at Thuckalay*		*Total*	
		No. of Members	*Percent-age*	*No. of Members*	*Percent-age*	*No. of Members*	*Percent-age*
1.	Less than 3	45	14.52	17	6.69	62	10.99
2.	3–4	95	30.65	72	28.35	167	29.61
3.	5–6	93	30.00	111	43.70	204	36.17
4.	7–8	41	13.23	33	12.99	74	13.12
5.	Above 8	36	11.61	21	8.27	57	10.11
	Total	310	100.00	254	100.00	564	100.00

Source: Primary Data.

Personal Income of the Members

The personal income of the members determines the purchasing power and the standard of living. It may have its own influence on the level of knowledge and awareness about the societies. So it is included as one of the profile variables in the present study. The personal income of the members was confined to less than Rs. 5,000, Rs. 5000 to 10,000; Rs. 10,001 to 15,000; Rs. 15,001 to 20,000 and more than Rs. 20,000 in the present study. The distribution of members on the basis of their personal income is shown in Table 4.8.

The important ranges of personal income among the members in the present study were Rs.10,001 to 15,000; Rs. 5000 to 10,000 and Rs. 15,001 to 20,000 which constitute 31.21, 23.05 and 21.45 per cent to the total respectively. The number of members who had a personal income of above Rs. 20,000 was 13.30 per cent to the total. In the societies at Nagercoil 30.32 and 22.58 per cent members had a personal income of Rs. 10,001 to Rs. 15,000 and

Rs. 15,001 to Rs. 20,000. Whereas in the societies at Thuckalay, 32.28 and 24.02 per cent members had a personal income of Rs. 10,001 to Rs. 15,000 and Rs. 5,000 to Rs. 10,000 respectively.

Table 4.8

Personal Income of the Members

Sl. No.	*Personal Income Per Month (Rs.)*	*Societies at Nagercoil*		*Societies at Thuckalay*		*Total*	
		No. of Members	*Percent-age*	*No. of Members*	*Percent-age*	*No. of Members*	*Percent-age*
1.	Less than 5000	34	10.97	28	11.02	62	10.99
2.	5000 – 10,000	69	22.26	61	24.02	130	23.05
3.	10001 – 15,000	94	30.32	82	32.28	176	31.21
4.	15001 – 20,000	70	22.58	51	20.08	121	21.45
5.	More than 20,000	43	13.87	32	12.60	75	13.30
	Total	310	100.00	254	100.00	564	100.00

Source: Primary Data.

Personality Traits of the Members

The personality traits of the members show their psychological aspects. Personality traits are the revelation of behaviour on various aspects among the members. In the present study, the personality traits of the members have been estimated with the help of the media exposure, sociability, innovativeness, credit orientation and scientific orientation among the members.

Media Exposure

The media exposure indicates their level of awareness and usage of various media among the members. In the present study, the media exposure has been measured with the help of some related statements. The statements of the members have been rated at five point scale by the members. The scores have been assigned on these scales. By the total score obtained by the members, their level of exposure have been determined. In the present study, the level of media exposure was confined to very high, high, moderate, low and very low.

Table 4.9
Media Exposure of the Members

Sl. No.	*Level of Media Exposure*	*Societies at Nagercoil*		*Societies at Thuckalay*		*Total*	
		No. of Members	*Percent-age*	*No. of Members*	*Percent-age*	*No. of Members*	*Percent-age*
1.	Very high	113	36.45	81	31.89	194	34.40
2.	High	82	26.45	74	29.13	156	27.66
3.	Moderate	58	18.71	55	21.65	113	20.04
4.	Low	40	12.90	36	14.17	76	13.48
5.	Very Low	17	5.48	8	3.15	25	4.43
	Total	310	100.00	254	100.00	564	100.00

Source: Primary Data.

Table 4.9 explains the levels of media exposure among the members. Among the members 34.40 and 27.66 per cent to the total respectively have very high and high media exposure. Members who have low and very low level in the media of exposure constitute 17.91 per cent each to the total. In societies at Nagercoil, the most important level of media exposure was very high which alone constitute 36.45 per cent to the total 310 members whereas in the societies at Thuckalay, it constitutes 31.89 per cent to its total. The analysis infers that the members in the present study were in high level of media exposure.

Sociability Among the Members

The sociability represents the level of interest and interaction of the members with various members and groups in the society. It is included as one of the personality traits variables. In the present study, the sociability among the members was calculated with the help of some relative statements which were measured at five point scale. The total score on the sociability among the members was taken to measure their level of sociability. In the present study, the level of sociability was classified into very high, high, moderate, low and very low.

Table 4.10

Sociability of the Members

Sl. No.	*Level of Sociability*	*Societies at Nagercoil*		*Societies at Thuckalay*		*Total*	
		No. of Members	*Percent-age*	*No. of Members*	*Percent-age*	*No. of Members*	*Percent-age*
1.	Very high	68	21.94	36	14.17	104	18.44
2.	High	71	22.90	47	18.50	118	20.92
3.	Moderate	83	26.77	88	34.65	171	30.32
4.	Low	50	16.13	62	24.41	112	19.86
5.	Very low	38	12.26	21	8.27	59	10.46
	Total	310	100.00	254	100.00	564	100.00

Source: Primary Data.

Table 4.10 exhibits the distribution of members on the basis of their level of sociability. The important levels of sociability were moderate, high and low which constitute 30.32, 20.92 and 19.86 per cent to the total respectively. Members who were at very high level in sociability constitute 18.44 per cent to the total. The levels of sociability among the members in societies at Nagercoil were moderate and high which constitute 26.77 and 22.90 per cent to the total whereas in societies at Thuckalay, these two were moderate and low which constitute 34.65 and 24.41 per cent to the total of 254 members.

Innovativeness of the Members

The innovativeness indicate the level of honouring, adopting and accepting the new things in life. Since the level of innovativeness determines the level of expectations and perceptions on the services offered by the societies, it is included in the present study. The level of innovativeness among the members was measured with the help of some related statements. The total score from all statements obtained by the members was used to determine their level of innovativeness. In the present study, their levels of innovativeness were confined to very high, high, moderate, low and very low. The distribution of members on the basis of their levels of innovativeness is shown in Table 4.11.

Table 4.11

Innovativeness of the Members

Sl. No.	*Level of Innovativeness*	*Societies at Nagercoil*		*Societies at Thuckalay*		*Total*	
		No. of Members	*Percent-age*	*No. of Members*	*Percent-age*	*No. of Members*	*Percent-age*
1.	Very high	27	8.71	17	6.69	44	7.80
2.	High	36	11.61	41	16.14	77	13.65
3.	Moderate	71	22.90	54	21.26	125	22.16
4.	Low	80	25.81	73	28.74	153	27.13
5.	Very Low	96	30.97	69	27.17	165	29.26
	Total	310	100.00	254	100.00	564	100.00

Source: Primary Data.

The levels of innovativeness among the majority of members were very low, low and moderate which constitute 29.26, 27.13 and 22.16 per cent to the total respectively. Members who had very high level in this aspect constitute 7.80 per cent to the total. In societies at Nagercoil, the levels of innovativeness among the members were very low and low. They constitute 30.97 and 25.81 per cent to its respective total of 310 members. In societies at Thuckalay, low and very low levels constitute 28.74 and 27.17 per cent to the respective total of 254 members.

Credit Orientation Among the Members

The credit orientation indicates the level of awareness, knowledge and understanding on the various aspects of credit and credit institution. The credit orientation is highly essential to mobilise, utilise and repay the credit among the members. The level of credit orientation among the members was measured with the help of some related statements. By the scores obtained by the members, their level of credit orientation was determined.

The levels of credit orientation were classified into very high, high, moderate, low and very low in the present study. The distribution of members on the basis of their level of credit orientation is shown in Table 4.12.

Table 4.12

Credit Orientation among the Members

Sl. No.	Level of Credit Orientation	Societies at Nagercoil		Societies at Thuckalay		Total	
		No. of Members	Percent-age	No. of Members	Percent-age	No. of Members	Percent-age
1.	Very high	42	13.55	23	9.06	65	11.52
2.	High	56	18.06	31	12.20	87	15.43
3.	Moderate	103	33.23	89	35.04	192	34.04
4.	Low	68	21.94	54	21.26	122	21.63
5.	Very Low	41	13.23	57	22.44	98	17.38
	Total	310	100.00	254	100.00	564	100.00

Source: Primary Data.

The important levels of credit orientation among the members were moderate, low and very low which constitute 34.04, 21.63 and 17.38 per cent to the total respectively. The members who had high and very high levels in this aspect constitute 26.95 per cent to the total. The first two important level of credit orientation among the members in the societies at Nagercoil were moderate and low which constitute 33.23 and 21.94 per cent to the total respectively. In the societies at Thuckalay, these two were moderate and very low levels constitute 35.04 and 22.44 per cent to the total of 254 members respectively.

Scientific Orientation of the Members

In the case of banking activities, the scientific orientation among the members is highly essential to mobilise the cheapest source of finance, optimum utilisation of finance and proper repayment of loans. The scientific orientation among the members was measured through some related statements at five point scale. The levels of scientific orientation were confined to very high, high, moderate, low and very low. The distribution of members on the basis of their scientific orientation is shown in Table 4.13.

Table 4.13

Scientific Orientation of the Members

Sl. No.	*Level of Scientific Orientation*	*Societies at Nagercoil*		*Societies at Thuckalay*		*Total*	
		No. of Members	*Percent-age*	*No. of Members*	*Percent-age*	*No. of Members*	*Percent-age*
1.	Very high	12	3.87	8	3.15	20	3.55
2.	High	16	5.16	13	5.12	29	5.14
3.	Moderate	73	23.55	69	27.17	142	25.18
4.	Low	108	34.84	54	21.26	162	28.72
5.	Very Low	101	32.58	110	43.31	211	37.41
	Total	310	100.00	254	100.00	564	100.00

Source: Primary Data.

The important levels of scientific orientation among the members were very low, low and moderate which constitute 37.41, 28.72 and 25.18 per cent to the total respectively. In the societies at Nagercoil, the members who were high and very high in scientific orientation constitute 9.03 per cent to its total of 310 members whereas in the societies at Thuckalay, they constitute 8.27 per cent to the total of 254 members. In total, the members who were at very low and low levels in scientific orientation constitute 67.42 per cent and 64.57 per cent to the respective total in the Nagercoil and Thuckalay societies.

PERSONALITY INDEX

The personality index represents the collective behaviour of the members. In the present study, the personality index was prepared by

$$PI = \frac{\sum SPV_i}{\sum MSPV_i} \times 100$$

Where PI = Personality Index

SPV = Score on the personality variables

MSPV = Maximum score on the personality variables.

In the present study, the variables included in the measurement of media exposure, sociability, innovativeness, credit orientation and scientific orientation among the members were treated as the personality variables. The personality index was confined to less than 20 per cent, 20 to 40, 41 to 60, 61 to 80 and above 80 per cent. The distribution of members on the basis of the personality index is shown in Table 4.14.

Table 4.14

Personality Index of the Members

Sl. No.	*Personality Index (in per cent)*	*Societies at Nagercoil*		*Societies at Thuckalay*		*Total*	
		No. of Members	*Percent-age*	*No. of Members*	*Percent-age*	*No. of Members*	*Percent-age*
1.	Less than 20	52	16.77	42	16.54	94	16.67
2.	20 – 40	79	25.49	68	26.77	147	26.06
3.	41 – 60	116	37.42	94	37.01	210	37.23
4.	61 – 80	42	13.55	39	15.35	81	14.36
5.	Above 80	21	6.77	11	4.33	32	5.67
	Total	310	100.00	254	100.00	564	100.00

The important personality indices among the members in the ranges 41 to 60 per cent, 20 to 40 per cent and less than 20 per cent constitute 37.23, 26.06 and 16.67 per cent to the total respectively. The number of members who had the personality index of above 80 per cent constitutes 5.67 per cent to the total. The first two important personality indices among the members of the societies at Nagercoil in the ranges 41 to 60 per cent and

20 to 40 per cent constitute 37.42 and 25.49 per cent to the total of 310 members. In the societies at Thuckalay, these two indices in the ranges 41 to 60 per cent and 20 to 40 per cent constitute 37.01 and 26.77 per cent to the total of 254 members.

FAMILY INCOME OF THE MEMBERS

The family income represents the total income earned by the earning members of the family. Since the family income is one of the important factors which determines the standard of living of the family and also influences the banking activities of the members, it is included as one of the profile variables. The family income per month of the members was classified into less than Rs. 6,000, Rs. 6,000 to 10,000; Rs. 10,001 to 14,000; Rs. 14,001 to 18,000; Rs. 18,001 to 22,000 and above Rs. 22,000. The distribution of members according to their family income is presented in Table 4.15.

Table 4.15

Family Income of the Members

Sl. No.	*Family Income Per Month*	*Societies at Nagercoil*		*Societies at Thuckalay*		*Total*	
		No. of Members	*Percentage*	*No. of Members*	*Percentage*	*No. of Members*	*Percentage*
1.	Less than 6000	39	12.58	23	9.06	62	10.99
2.	6000 – 10,000	54	17.42	47	18.50	101	17.91
3.	10001 – 14,000	89	28.71	61	24.02	150	26.59
4.	14001 – 18,000	62	20.00	72	28.35	134	23.76
5.	18001 – 22,000	34	10.97	23	9.06	57	10.11
6.	Above 22,000	32	10.32	28	11.02	60	10.64
	Total	310	100.00	254	100.00	564	100.00

Source: Primary Data.

Totally, 68.26 per cent of the members were in the range from Rs.6000 to 18,000 family income per month. The most common family income ranges of the members were Rs. 10,001 to 14,000 and Rs. 14,001 to 18,000. They constitute 26.59 and 23.76 per cent to the total respectively. Members who had a family income of above Rs. 22,000 per month constitute 10.64 per cent to the total. In societies at Nagercoil, the common family income ranges were Rs. 10,001 to 14,000 and Rs. 14,001 to 18,000 whereas in societies at Thuckalay, they were Rs. 14,001 to 18,000 and Rs. 10,001 to 14,000.

MONTHLY EXPENDITURES OF THE MEMBERS

The monthly expenditures of the members indicate their personal commitment to the family per month. It has its own impact on savings and also on the indebtedness among the members. The monthly expenditures of the members in the present study were confined to less than Rs. 6,000; Rs. 6,000 to 10,000; Rs. 10,001 to 14,000; Rs. 14,001 to 18,000 and above Rs. 18,000. The distribution of respondents on the basis of their monthly expenditures is exhibited in Table 4.16.

Table 4.16

Monthly Expenditures of the Members

Sl. No.	*Monthly Expenditure (Rs.)*	*Societies at Nagercoil*		*Societies at Thuckalay*		*Total*	
		No. of Members	*Percent-age*	*No. of Members*	*Percent-age*	*No. of Members*	*Percent-age*
1.	Less than 6,000	31	10.00	17	6.69	48	8.51
2.	6000 – 10,000	49	15.81	42	16.54	91	16.13
3.	10001 – 14,000	86	27.74	54	21.26	140	24.82
4.	14001 – 18,000	73	23.55	110	43.31	183	32.45
5.	Above 18,000	71	22.90	31	12.20	102	18.09
	Total	310	100.00	254	100.00	564	100.00

Source: Primary Data.

Members with the monthly expenditure of Rs.14,001 to Rs. 18,000 constitutes 32.45 per cent to the total. Those in the expenditure range of Rs. 10,001 to Rs. 14,000 constitute 24.82 per cent to the total. In the societies at Nagercoil, members with monthly expenditures of Rs. 10,001 to Rs. 14,000 constitute 27.74

per cent to the total. In the societies at Thuckalay, those in the range Rs.14,001 to Rs.18,000 constitute 43.31 per cent to the total.

MONTHLY SAVINGS OF THE MEMBERS

The monthly savings represent the difference between the total income and expenditure per month. The monthly savings of the members were confined to less than Rs.1,000; Rs. 1,000 to 2,000; Rs. 2,001 to 3,000; Rs. 3,001 to 4,000 and above Rs. 4,000. The distribution of respondents according to their monthly savings is illustrated in Table 4.17.

Table 4.17

Monthly Savings of the Members

Sl. No.	Monthly Savings	Societies at Nagercoil		Societies at Thuckalay		Total	
		No. of Members	Percent-age	No. of Members	Percent-age	No. of Members	Percent-age
1.	Less than 1000	69	22.26	32	12.60	101	17.91
2.	1000 – 2000	86	27.74	67	26.38	153	27.13
3.	2001 – 3000	43	13.87	41	16.14	84	14.89
4.	3001 – 4000	47	15.16	53	20.87	100	17.73
5.	Above 4000	65	20.97	61	24.02	126	22.34
	Total	310	100.00	254	100.00	564	100.00

Source: Primary Data.

Members with monthly savings of Rs.1,000-Rs. 2,000 and above Rs. 4,000 constitute 27.13 and 22.34 per cent to the total respectively. The members who have saved less than Rs. 1,000 per month constitute 17.91 per cent to the total. In the societies at Nagercoil, members with the monthly savings Rs. 1,000 to 2,000 alone constitute 27.74 per cent to the total. In societies at Thuckalay, those with the monthly savings of Rs. 1,000 to 2,000 constitute 26.38 per cent to the total.

Ways of Savings of the Members

In general, the ways of savings of the members are too many. In the present study, the ways of savings of the members were confined to Life Insurance, Provident Fund, Bank Deposits, Thrift Societies, Private Chits and National Savings Certificate. The members were asked to mention their ways of savings. Since the multi response was allowed, the members who had invested in different saving schemes are shown in Table 4.18.

Table 4.18

Ways of Savings of the Members

Sl. No.	*Ways of Savings*	*Societies at Nagercoil*		*Societies at Thuckalay*		*Total*	
		No. of Members	*Percent-age*	*No. of Members*	*Percent-age*	*No. of Members*	*Percent-age*
1.	Life Insurance	268	86.45	117	46.06	385	68.26
2.	Provident Fund	276	89.03	203	79.92	479	84.93
3.	Bank Deposits	196	63.23	131	51.57	327	57.98
4.	ECTCS	310	100.00	254	100.00	564	100.00
5.	Private Chits	89	28.71	68	26.77	157	27.84
6.	National Savings Certificate	46	14.84	24	9.45	70	12.41

Source: Primary Data.

The important ways of savings of the members was ECTCS, followed by provident fund and life insurance which constitute 84.93 and 68.26 per cent to the total respectively. The other ways of savings were bank deposits and private chits which constitute 57.98 and 27.84 per cent to the total respectively. Apart from the ECTCS, the other two important ways of savings among the members in the societies at Nagercoil were provident fund and life insurance which constitute 89.03 and 86.45 per cent to the total. In societies at Thuckalay, these two were provident fund and bank deposits which constitute 79.92 and 51.57 per cent to the total respectively.

ASSETS POSITION OF THE MEMBERS

Since the assets position of the members is very important in the repayment behaviour of the borrowers, it is included as one of the profile variables. The value of assets owned by the respondents in the present study was confined to less than Rs. 5 lakhs, Rs. 5 to 10, Rs. 11 to 15, Rs. 16 to 20 and above Rs. 20 lakh. The number of respondents under different assets position are shown in Table 4.19.

Table 4.19

Total Assets Position of the Members

Sl. No.	*Value of Assets (Rs. in Lakh)*	*Societies at Nagercoil*		*Societies at Thuckalay*		*Total*	
		No. of Members	*Percent-age*	*No. of Members*	*Percent-age*	*No. of Members*	*Percent-age*
1.	Less than 5	80	25.81	63	24.80	143	25.35
2.	5 – 10	74	23.87	68	26.77	142	25.18
3.	11 – 15	69	22.26	74	29.13	143	25.35
4.	16 – 20	52	16.77	32	12.60	84	14.89
5.	Above 20	35	11.29	17	6.69	52	9.22
	Total	310	100.00	254	100.00	564	100.00

Source: Primary Data.

Members with the value of assets from Rs. 11 to 15 lakh; less than Rs. 5 lakh and Rs. 5 to 10 lakh constitute 25.35; 25.35 and 25.18 per cent to the total respectively. The members of the societies at Nagercoil, with the value of assets less than Rs. 5 lakh constitute 25.81 per cent to the total whereas in societies at Thuckalay, those with the asset values of Rs. 11 to 15 lakh constitute 29.13 per cent to the total.

TOTAL LIABILITIES OF THE MEMBERS

The total liabilities of the members in the present study were classified into less than Rs. 5 lakhs, Rs. 5 to 10 lakhs, Rs. 11 to 15 lakhs, Rs. 16 to 20 lakh and above Rs. 20 Lakh. The liabilities of the members are shown in Table 4.20.

Table 4.20

Total Liabilities of the Members

Sl. No.	*Total Liabilities (Rs. in Lakh)*	*Societies at Nagercoil*		*Societies at Thuckalay*		*Total*	
		No. of Members	*Percen-tage*	*No. of Members*	*Percen-tage*	*No. of Members*	*Percen-tage*
1.	Less than 5	143	46.13	102	40.16	245	43.44
2.	5 – 10	43	13.87	62	24.41	105	18.62
3.	11 – 15	61	19.68	47	18.50	108	19.15
4.	16 – 20	27	8.71	21	8.27	48	8.51
5.	Above 20	36	11.61	22	8.66	58	10.28
	Total	310	100.00	254	100.00	564	100.00

Source: Primary Data.

The members with the liabilities less than Rs. 5 lakh, Rs. 11 to 15 lakh and Rs. 5 to 10 lakh which constitute 43.44; 19.15 and 18.62 per cent to the total members respectively. The members in societies at Nagercoil, with the liabilities less than Rs. 5 lakh and Rs. 11 to 15 lakh constitute 46.13 and 19.68 per cent to the total of 310 respondents respectively. In the societies at Thuckalay, those with liabilities less than Rs. 5 lakh and Rs. 5 to 10 lakh constitute 40.16 and 24.41 per cent to the total of 254 respondents respectively.

Sources of Borrowings

The sources of borrowings of the members are several. In the present study, the sources were confined to banks, private moneylenders, chit-funds, ECTCS and friends and relatives. Since, the respondents are having more than one source of borrowings, the members were asked to mention their sources of borrowings. The sources of borrowings and the members who have utilised the different sources are illustrated in Table 4.21.

Table 4.21
Sources of Borrowings

Sl. No.	*Sources of Borrowings*	*Societies at Nagercoil*		*Societies at Thuckalay*		*Total*	
		No. of Members	*Percent-age*	*No. of Members*	*Percent-age*	*No. of Members*	*Percent-age*
1.	Banks	114	36.77	108	42.52	122	21.63
2.	Private Moneylenders	99	31.94	84	33.07	183	32.45
3.	Chit-funds	136	43.87	106	41.73	242	42.91
4.	E.C.T.C.S	242	78.06	183	72.05	425	75.35
5.	Friends and Relatives	68	21.94	48	18.90	116	20.57
	Total	310	100.00	254	100.00	564	100.00

Source: Primary Data.

The important sources of borrowings of the members were chit-funds and private moneylenders apart from the ECTCS The above two sources of borrowings constitute 42.91 and 32.45 per cent to the total respectively. Among the members in societies at Nagercoil, the most important source of borrowings apart from the E.C.T.C.S was the chit-funds which alone constitutes 43.87 per cent to the total. In the societies at Thuckalay, it was banks which constitutes 42.52 per cent to the total respectively.

Duration of Membership

The duration of membership represents the number of years the respondents are the members of the society. Since the years of membership give more exposure and knowledge of the societies, it is also included as one of the profile variables. The duration of membership was confined to less than 5 years, 5 to 8 years, 9 to 12 years, 13 to 15 years and more than 15 years. The distribution of members on the basis of their duration of membership is shown in Table 4.22.

Table 4.22
Duration of Membership in the Societies

Sl. No.	*Years of Membership*	*Societies at Nagercoil*		*Societies at Thuckalay*		*Total*	
		No. of Members	*Percentage*	*No. of Members*	*Percentage*	*No. of Members*	*Percentage*
1.	Less than 5 years	21	6.77	17	6.69	38	6.74
2.	5 – 8 years	42	13.55	32	12.60	74	13.12
3.	9 – 12 years	53	17.10	41	16.14	94	16.67
4.	13 – 15 years	89	28.71	33	12.99	122	21.63
5.	More than 15 years	105	33.87	131	51.57	236	41.84
	Total	310	100.00	254	100.00	564	100.00

Source: Primary Data.

The duration of membership of the members, with more than 15 years constitutes 41.84 per cent to the total. The number of members with the duration of less than 5 years constitutes 6.74 per cent to the total. In the societies at Nagercoil, the duration of membership with more than 15 years constitutes 33.87 per cent to the total members. In the case of societies at Thuckalay, this was 51.57 per cent to the total of 254 members.

REASONS FOR HAVING MEMBERSHIP IN THE SOCIETY

The employees of the various organisations have joined as the members of the societies with various expectations. The reasons for joining as the member of the society are too many. In the present study, these reasons were confined to availability of loan, easy monthly instalment, low rate of interest, easy formalities, deduction at source, persuasion, accessibility, influence of union, words-of-mouth, savings possibility, assurance, reliability, responsiveness, courtesy, accuracy of accounts, less time consuming, high rate of dividend, high interest on deposits and amount of loan (Jain, PK, 2000).[1] The members were asked to rate the above said reasons at five point scale namely highly important, important, moderate, not important and not at all important. The marks assigned on these scales were 5, 4, 3, 2 and 1 respectively.

Narration of the Reasons Leading to have Membership

The mean scores of the reasons to have membership in the societies have been computed. The 't' test was administered to find out the significant differences among the members of the societies at Nagercoil and Thuckalay, regarding their views on various reasons to have membership in the societies. The resulted mean scores and the respective 't' statistics are shown in Table 4.23.

Table 4.23

Mean Scores of Various Reasons to have Membership in the Societies

Sl. No.	*Reasons*	*Mean Score*		*'t' Statistics*
		Societies at Nagercoil	*Societies at Thuckalay*	
1.	Availability of loan	3.9108	2.8641	3.7182*
2.	Higher monthly instalment	3.7022	3.0233	1.6696
3.	Low rate of interest	3.6041	2.6142	2.8081*
4.	Easy formalities	4.1676	3.1143	3.0241*
5.	Deduction at source	3.7063	3.6926	0.4508
6.	Persuasion	2.5021	3.6244	-3.1141*
7.	Accessibility	2.8663	4.0111	-3.6693*
8.	Influence of union	2.4408	3.9908	-3.9082*
9.	Oral opinion	3.1143	3.8089	-1.7031
10.	Saving possibility	2.6075	3.6358	-2.6334*
11.	Assurance	3.8998	2.8081	2.8091*
12.	Reliability	4.1144	3.0676	2.9089*
13.	Responsiveness	3.9906	2.7212	3.1199*
14.	Courteous	3.9763	3.0963	2.2317*
15.	Accuracy of accounts	3.6069	3.4388	0.6049
16.	Less time consuming	4.2266	3.1482	3.1802*
17.	High rate of dividend	3.3301	2.9803	0.6164
18.	High interest on deposits	2.6041	3.0347	-0.5942
19.	Amount of loan	2.8087	2.5863	0.6087

* Significant at five per cent level.

The important reasons to have a membership in the societies at Nagercoil were less time consuming, easy formalities and reliability since the respective mean scores were 4.2266, 4.1676 and 4.1144. Among the members in the societies at Thuckalay these reasons were accessibility, influence of union and oral opinion since its mean scores were 4.0111, 3.9908 and 3.8089 respectively. Regarding the perceptions on various reasons, the significant differences among the members in the groups of societies have been identified in the case of availability of loan, low rate of interest, easy formalities, persuasion, accessibility, influence of union, saving possibility, assurance, reliability, responsiveness, courteous and lesser time consuming since the respective 't' statistics were significant at five percent level.

In order to narrate the reasons for having membership in a society, the factor analysis was administered. The scores of the various reasons were taken into account for the analysis. The factor analysis revealed four important factors for having a membership in the society. They were product, promotion, service quality and finance factor. The reasons for each factor and the factor loadings are given in Table 4.24.

The narrated four factors leading to have a membership in the society explain the various reasons to have a membership, to the extent of 66.72 per cent. The most important factor was 'Product' factor which consists of five reasons with the reliability coefficient of 0.8184. The Eigen value and the per cent of variation explained by this factor were 4.0182 and 21.38 per cent respectively. The second and third important factors were 'Promotion' and 'Service Quality' factors with the Eigen values of 3.1409 and 2.4693 respectively. The most important reasons included in the promotion and service quality were persuasion and assurance respectively. These two factors explain the variables leading to have a membership at society to the extent of 19.27 and 15.36 per cent respectively.

The last factor narrated by the factor analysis was finance factor. It consists of three reasons with the reliability coefficient of 0.7231. The Eigen value and the per cent of variation of this factor were 1.8114 and 10.71 per cent to the total. The most important reason in this factor was high rate of dividend. To sum up, the factor analysis results in four important factors persuading the employees to have a membership at a society. These four factors were considered for further analysis. The scores of the factors were drawn from the mean scores of various reasons in each factor.

Table 4.24

Factor Loading of Various Reasons to have a Membership in the Societies

Factors (Eigen Value)	*Reasons*	*Factor Loading*	*Reliability Coefficient*	*Per cent of Variation*
Product (4.0182)	Availability of Loan	.8904	0.8184	21.38
	Higher Monthly Instalment	.8631		
	Low Rate of Interest	.7345		
	Easy formalities	.6271		
	Deduction at Source	.6088		
Promotion (3.1409)	Persuasion	.9141	0.8607	19.27
	Accessibility	.8302		
	Influence of Union	.7636		
	Oral opinion	.6814		
	Savings possibility	.6091		
Service Quality (2.4693)	Assurance	.8824	0.8918	15.36
	Reliability	.8163		
	Responsiveness	.7908		
	Courteous	.7362		
	Accuracy of Accounts	.7083		
	Less time consuming	.6506		
Finance (1.8114)	High rate of dividend	.8372	0.7231	10.71
	High interest on deposits	.7908		
	Amount of Loan	.6071		

Perception on Important Factors

In order to exhibit the important reasons to enrol as a member of the society, the mean scores of the perception on four important factors have been calculated. To analyse the significant difference among the members in two groups of societies regarding their perception on the important factors, the 't' test has been administered. The resulted mean scores of the factors and the respective 't' statistics are presented in Table 4.25.

Table 4.25

Perception on Important Factors

Sl. No.	*Factors*	*Mean Score*		*'t'-Statistics*
		Societies at Nagercoil	*Societies at Thuckalay*	
1.	Product	3.8182	3.0617	2.2306*
2.	Promotion	2.7062	3.8142	-3.1194*
3.	Service Quality	3.9691	3.0467	2.7086*
4.	Finance	2.9143	2.8671	0.3134

* Significant at 5 per cent level.

The highly perceived factors to join as a member of the societies at Nagercoil were 'Service Quality' and 'Product' factor since the mean scores were 3.9691 and 3.8182 respectively. In societies at Thuckalay, these two were 'Promotion' and 'Product' since the respective mean scores were 3.8142 and 3.0617. Regarding the perception on the important factors leading to have a membership in a society, the significant difference was noticed among the members in two groups of societies in the perception on product, promotion and service quality factor since the respective 't' statistics were significant at 5 per cent level.

Association Between the Profile of Respondents and their Perception on Factors

Since the profile of the respondents has its own impact on their perception on the factors leading to join as a member of the society, an attempt was made to analyse the profile of respondents and their perception on the factors. The included profile variables were gender, age, level of education, occupation, marital status, family size, personal income, family income and personality index. The one way analysis of variance was used to exhibit the association between the profile of respondents and their perception on important factors. The resulted 'F' statistics are presented in Table 4.26.

Table 4.26

Association Between the Profile of Members and their View on Important Reasons

Sl. No.	*Profile Variables*	*F-Statistics*			
		Product	*Promotion*	*Service Quality*	*Finance*
1.	Gender	2.9186	3.0672	4.2176*	3.9163*
2.	Age	1.9806	2.1143*	3.0671*	1.8604
3.	Level of Education	2.0811	2.7606*	1.3696	2.0417
4.	Occupation	2.1144	2.0896	2.5149*	2.6163*
5.	Marital Status	2.2081	1.8684	2.0709	2.1143
6.	Family Size	2.1086	1.9017	2.1183	2.4574*
7.	Personal Income	3.0842*	2.5608*	2.4086*	1.8408
8.	Family Income	2.4069*	2.8687*	2.9239*	2.0686
9.	Personality Index	3.01147*	2.4081*	3.3399*	2.6081*

* Significant at 5 per cent level.

Regarding the perception on 'product' factor, the significantly associating profile variables were personal income, family income and personality index since the respective 'F' statistics were significant at 5 per cent level. Regarding the perception on 'promotion' factor, the significant profile variables were age, level of education, personal income, family income and personality index. Regarding the perception on the 'service quality' factor, the significant difference among the members was identified when they were classified on the basis of gender, age, occupation, personal income, family income and personality index. Regarding the perception on 'finance' factor, the significantly associating profile variables were gender, occupation, family size and personality index since the respective 'F' statistics were significant at 5 per cent level.

DEPOSITS OF THE MEMBERS

It represents the members' deposits in the society on recurring basis. The accumulated deposits may vary from person to person. It also depends upon the duration of membership and the regularity in payment of deposits. The accumulated deposits in the society were classified into less than Rs. 20,000; Rs. 20,000 to 40,000; Rs. 40,001 to 60,000; Rs. 60,001 to 80,000 and above Rs. 80,000. The distribution of members on the basis of their deposits is shown in Table 4.27.

Table 4.27

Amount of Deposits of the Members

Sl. No.	*Amount of Deposits*	*Societies at Nagercoil*		*Societies at Thuckalay*		*Total*	
		No. of Members	*Percent-age*	*No. of Members*	*Percent-age*	*No. of Members*	*Percent-age*
1.	Less than 20,000	63	20.32	42	16.54	105	18.62
2.	20,000 – 40,000	84	27.10	59	23.23	143	25.35
3.	40001 – 60,000	71	22.90	68	26.77	139	24.65
4.	60001 – 80,000	58	18.71	56	22.05	114	20.21
5.	Above 80,000	34	10.97	29	11.42	63	11.17
	Total	310	100.00	254	100.00	564	100.00

Source: Primary Data.

The common ranges of deposits made by the members were Rs. 20,000 to 40,000 and Rs. 40,001 to 60,000, which constitute 25.35 and 24.65 per cent to the total respectively. The members who had an accumulated deposits of above Rs. 80,000 constitute 11.17 per cent to the total. In the societies at Nagercoil, the first two common ranges of deposits among the members were Rs. 20,000 to 40,000 and Rs. 40,001 to 60,000, which constitute 27.10 and 22.90 per cent to the total respectively. In the societies at Thuckalay, these two were Rs. 40,001 to 60,000 and Rs. 20,000 to 40,000, which constitute 26.77 and 23.23 per cent to the total respectively.

Reasons for Depositing in the Societies

The members save their money in the ECTCS for several reasons. In order to identify the important reasons for depositing money at the society, the present study confines the reasons to high rate of interest, salary deduction, safety, savings promotion, feeling of cooperation, influence of union and accessibility. The members were asked to rate the above said reasons at five point scale with options from highly agree to highly disagree which consists of marks from 5 to 1 respectively. The mean scores of the reasons have been computed and given in Table 4.28.

Table 4.28

Reasons for Depositing in the Societies

Sl. No.	*Reasons*	*Mean Score*		*'t-Statistics*
		Societies at Nagercoil	*Societies at Thuckalay*	
1.	High rate of interest	2.4517	3.0217	– 1.8104
2.	Salary deduction	3.8603	3.0403	2.1472*
3.	Safety	2.3108	2.7674	– 0.7641
4.	Savings Promotion	3.4542	2.8186	1.4037
5.	Feeling of Cooperation	2.9091	2.0406	2.0804*
6.	Influence of Union	3.8181	2.5672	3.1147*
7.	Accessibility	2.4342	3.6171	-3.2342*

* Significant at 5 per cent level.

The important reasons to deposit money at the society by the members in the societies at Nagercoil were salary deduction and influence of union since the respective mean scores were 3.8603 and 3.8181. In the societies at Thuckalay, the two important reasons were accessibility and salary deduction since its mean scores were 3.6171 and 3.0403 respectively. Regarding the perception on the reasons for depositing at the society, the significant difference was noticed among the members in two groups of societies in the perception on salary deduction, feeling of cooperation, influence of union and accessibility since the respective 't' statistics were significant at five per cent level.

LOANS BORROWED FROM THE SOCIETIES

The members of societies may borrow loans according to their needs. Out of 564 selected members in the present study, only 425 have borrowed loans from the ECTCS In societies at Nagercoil, the percentage of selected members who have borrowed loans constitutes 78.06 per cent to the total of 310 members. In societies at Thuckalay, it constitutes 72.05 per cent to the total of 254 members. Since the members borrow different quantum of loan amounts from the society, the loans borrowed were confined to less than Rs. 30,000; Rs. 30,000 to 60,000; Rs. 60,001 to 90,000; Rs. 90,001 to 1,20,000 and above Rs. 1,20,000. The distribution of members according to their loan amount borrowed from the society is given in Table 4.29.

Table 4.29

Loans Borrowed from the Societies

Sl. No.	*Loans borrowed*	*Societies at Nagercoil*		*Societies at Thuckalay*		*Total*	
		No. of Members	*Percent-age*	*No. of Members*	*Percent-age*	*No. of Members*	*Percent-age*
1.	Less than 30,000	32	13.22	42	22.95	74	17.41
2.	30,000 – 60,000	66	27.27	24	13.11	90	21.18
3.	60,001 – 90,000	83	34.30	69	37.70	152	35.76
4.	90,001 – 1,20,000	48	19.83	37	20.22	85	20.00
5.	Above 1.2 lakhs	13	5.37	11	6.01	24	5.65
	Total	242	100.00	183	100.00	425	100.00

Source: Primary Data.

35.76 per cent of members availed of the loan amount of Rs. 60,001 to 90,000. The number of members who have borrowed a loan amount of above Rs. 1.2 lakh constitutes only 5.65 per cent to the total. In societies at Nagercoil, 34.30 per cent of members availed of the loan from Rs. 60,000 to 90,000. In societies at Thuckalay, 37.70 per cent to the total 183 members borrowed between Rs. 60,001 to 90,000.

Purpose of Loan Borrowed form the Societies

The members borrow money from the societies for different purposes. The members were asked to mention the purpose of their loan. Members borrowed loans for different purposes are summarised in Table 4.30.

Table 4.30

Purposes of Loan Borrowed from the Societies

Sl. No.	*Purposes of Loan*	*Societies at Nagercoil*		*Societies at Thuckalay*		*Total*	
		No. of Members	*Percent-age*	*No. of Members*	*Percent-age*	*No. of Members*	*Percent-age*
1.	Children's Education	86	35.54	71	38.80	157	36.94
2.	Marriage	62	25.62	42	22.95	104	24.47
3.	Purchasing of Assets	32	13.22	34	18.58	66	15.53
4.	Repayment of other Debts	29	11.98	25	13.66	54	12.71
5.	Others	33	13.64	11	6.01	44	10.35
	Total	242	100.00	183	100.00	425	100.00

Source: Primary Data.

The important purposes of loan borrowed from the societies by the members were children's education and marriage which constitute 36.94 and 24.47 per cent to the total respectively. Totally, 12.71 per cent of the members borrowed loan for the purpose of repayment of other debts. 35.54 and 25.62 per cent of the total of 242 members of the societies at Nagercoil borrowed loans for children's education and marriage. 38.80 and 22.95 per cent of the total of 183 members of the societies at Thuckalay borrowed loans for the same purposes.

Difficulties Encountered in Getting Loans

The borrowers of loans may encounter many problems and difficulties in getting loans from the society. Even though, the difficulties are too many, the present study confined to insufficient loan amount, higher rate of interest, procedural formalities, high processing time, time taken to disburse the loan, equal monthly instalment, repayment period, guarantor's certificate, salary deduction and employer's certificate. The borrowers were asked to rate the above said problems at five point scale with the options highly serious, serious, moderate, not serious and not at all serious. The scores assigned to these options in their order were 5, 4, 3, 2 and 1 respectively. The mean score was calculated to exhibit the importance of difficulties in getting loans.

Table 4.31

Difficulties Encountered in Getting Loans

Sl. No.	*Difficulties*	*Mean Score*		*'t'-Statistics*
		Societies at Nagercoil	*Societies at Thuckalay*	
1.	Insufficient Loan Amount	3.2162	3.3862	-0.3192
2.	Higher Rate of Interest	2.4037	3.1661	-2.3408*
3.	Procedural Formalities	3.6168	2.1918	2.9697*
4.	High Processing Time	2.7073	3.2617	-0.8986
5.	Time taken to Disburse the Loan	2.4142	2.8681	-0.7033
6.	Higher Monthly Instalment	3.6902	2.8019	2.1147*
7.	Repayment Period	3.7814	2.9133	2.8609*
8.	Guarantor's Certificate	2.4593	3.2676	-1.4084
9.	Salary Deduction	2.3314	2.6861	-0.4182
10.	Employers' Certificate	2.8682	2.5089	0.5019

* Significant at 5 per cent level.

Table 4.31 explains the mean score of various problems and the respective 't' statistics. The highly viewed problems for the members in societies at Nagercoil were repayment period, higher monthly instalment and procedural formalities since their mean scores were 3.7814, 3.6902 and 3.6168 respectively. In societies at Thuckalay, these were insufficient loan amount, guarantor's certificate and high processing time since the respective mean scores were 3.3862, 3.2676 and 3.2617. Regarding the different perceptions on problems, the significant differences among the members in two groups of societies were identified regarding the perceptions on higher rate of interest, procedural formalities, higher monthly instalment and repayment period since the respective 't' statistics were significant at five per cent level.

NATURE OF REPAYMENT

The nature of repayment by the members indicates the members' attitude to repay their loan to the society. The various natures of repayment were classified as regular, try to be a regular, irregular and long overdue. The distribution of members on the basis of their repayment behaviour is presented in Table 4.32.

Table 4.32

Nature of Repayment of Loan by the Members

Sl. No.	*Nature of Repayment*	*Societies at Nagercoil*		*Societies at Thuckalay*		*Total*	
		No. of Members	*Percent-age*	*No. of Members*	*Percent-age*	*No. of Members*	*Percent-age*
1.	Regular	103	42.56	72	39.34	175	41.18
2.	Try to be regular	52	21.49	28	15.30	80	18.82
3.	Irregular	44	18.18	47	25.68	91	21.41
4.	Long Overdue	43	17.77	36	19.67	79	18.59
	Total	242	100.00	183	100.00	425	100.00

Source: Primary Data.

The two important natures of repayment among the members were regular and irregular which constitute 41.18 and 21.41 per cent to the total respectively. In the societies at Nagercoil the regular repayers of loans were found to be 42.56 per cent of the total borrowers, whereas in societies at Thuckalay, it constitutes 39.34 per cent to the total. In total, the number of members who were trying to be regular constitute 18.82 per cent to the total.

REASONS FOR DEFAULTS AMONG THE MEMBERS

The default in repayment of loans by the members may be due to different reasons. In the present study, the reasons for defaults were confined to higher rate of interest, family problems, no penal rate, higher indebtedness, insufficient loan amount, leniency in recovery, higher monthly instalment, improper utilisation of loan, education expenditure, unexpected sickness, influence of co-workers, political influence, unexpected financial problems, management of debts and expectation to write off. The members were asked to rate the above said 15 reasons at five point scale with option from highly agree to highly disagree. The scores assigned on these scales were 5, 4, 3, 2 and 1 respectively. The mean scores for the different reasons and the 't' statistics revealing the significance of the differences among the opinions revealed by the members of the societies at Nagercoil and Thuckalay are given in Table 4.33.

Table 4.33 reveals the perceptions on the reasons for default in repayment. The significant differences among the borrowers' opinion in two groups of societies were identified with the help of 't' test. In the societies at Nagercoil, the important reasons for default were mismanagement of debts and unexpected financial problem since their respective means were 4.1173 and 4.0633. In societies at Thuckalay, these reasons were unexpected financial problem and higher monthly instalment since the mean scores were 3.9092 and 3.8681 respectively. Among the various reasons for defaults, the significant differences between the opinions of the members of the societies at Nagercoil and Thuckalay were identified to be the perceptions on family problems, leniency in recovery, higher monthly instalment, unexpected sickness, mismanagement of debts and expectation to write off since the respective 't' statistics were significant at 5 per cent level.

Table 4.33

Reasons for Defaults among the Members

Sl. No.	*Reasons for Defaults*	*Mean Score in*		*'t'-Statistics*
		Societies at Nagercoil	*Societies at Thuckalay*	
1.	Higher Rate of Interest	2.7139	2.5038	0.3086
2.	Family Problems	3.6814	2.5411	2.7314*
3.	No Penal Rate	3.4046	3.5167	-0.2673
4.	Higher Indebtedness	2.8187	3.0814	-0.3149
5.	Insufficient Loan Amount	3.0149	3.1718	-0.1983
6.	Leniency in Recovery	3.6033	2.4144	2.8018*
7.	Higher monthly instalment	2.7182	3.8681	-2.9394*
8.	Improper Utilisation of Loan	3.4686	2.9644	0.7867
9.	Education Expenditure	3.6808	3.5717	0.1023
10.	Unexpected Sickness	2.4951	3.5109	-2.1766*
11.	Influence of Co-workers	2.9892	2.6331	0.6891
12.	Political Influence	3.9091	3.4418	0.5517
13.	Unexpected Financial Problem	4.0633	3.9092	0.3039
14.	Mismanagement of Debts	4.1173	2.8996	2.8661*
15.	Expectation to Write Off	3.8914	3.0762	2.0411*

* Significant at 5 per cent level.

Narration of the Perception on Various Reasons for Defaults

The reasons for default, among the members were narrated with the help of factor analysis. The scores on various reasons for defaults in repayment by the members were included for this analysis. The resulted factors, variables in factors, their factor loading, reliability coefficient and the per cent of variation of the factors are shown in Table 4.34.

Table 4.34

Factors Loading of Various Reasons for Defaults

Factors (Eigen Value)	*Reasons for Overdue*	*Factor Loading*	*Reliability Coefficient*	*Per cent of Variation*
Environmental Factor (3.7109)	No penal rate	.8314	.8371	26.32
	Leniency in recovery	.7802		
	Expectation to Write off	.7119		
	Political Influence	.6306		
	Influence of Co-workers	.5917		
Financial Factor (3.0634)	Insufficient Loan Amount	.9114	.7308	21.27
	Educational Expenditure	.8606		
	Unexpected financial problem	.7263		
	Higher Monthly Instalment	.6508		
	Higher rate of interest	.5803		
Personal Factor (2.4173)	Family problems	.9332	.7661	19.08
	Improper utilisation of loan	.8606		
	Higher indebtedness	.7343		
	Unexpected sickness	.6802		
	Mismanagement of Debts	.5917		

The factor analysis narrated the fifteen reasons into three important factors namely 'Environmental', 'Financial' and 'Personal' factors. All these three factors explained the reasons for default by the members to the extent of 66.67 per cent. The most important factor was 'Environmental factor'. It consists of five reasons with the reliability coefficient of 0.8371. The Eigen value and the per cent of variation of this factor were 3.7109 and 26.32 per cent respectively. The second important factor was the 'Financial' factor which consists of five reasons with the reliability coefficient of 0.7308. The Eigen value and the per cent of variation were 3.0634 and 21.27 per cent respectively. The third important factor was the 'Personal' factor which consists of five reasons with the reliability coefficient of 0.7661. The Eigen value and the per cent of variation were 2.4173 and 19.08 per cent respectively. The important reasons in the above said three factors were no penal rate, insufficient loan amount and family problems respectively. The factor analysis results in three important factors (reasons) for default among the members namely environmental, financial and personal factor. The scores of the above said three factors were drawn from the mean scores of the variables in each factor.

Impact of Important Factors on Defaults Among the Members

The study has made an attempt to analyse the impact of important factors (reasons) on defaults among the members. In order to analyse this impact, the multiple regression analysis has been administered. The scores on the three important factors are taken as the score of the independent variables whereas the total amount of overdue is taken as the score of dependent variable. The fitted regression model is

$$y = a+b_1x_1+b_2x_2+b_3x_3+e$$

whereas y = Total amount of overdue among the respondents

x_1 = Score on Environmental factor among the respondents

x_2 = Score on Financial factor among the respondents

x_3 = Score on Personal factor among the respondents

$b_1, b_2, b_3,$ = Regression coefficients of independent variables

a = Intercept and

e = Error term.

The impact analysis is carried out among defaulters in the societies at Nagercoil, Thuckalay and also with the pooled data separately. The resulted regression coefficients of the independent variables are presented in Table 4.35.

Table 4.35

Impact of the Important Factors on Defaults among the Members

Sl. No.	*Factors*	*Regression Co-efficient*		
		Societies at Nagercoil	*Societies at Thuckalay*	*Pooled*
1.	Environmental Factor	.1082	.0897	0.1123
2.	Financial Factor	.5819*	.3981*	0.4087*
3.	Personal Factor	.3036*	.2445*	0.2962*
	Constant	1.4503	1.8089	1.6026
	R^2	0.7302	0.6861	0.7989
	F Statistics	11.6261*	9.7076*	12.6803*

* Significant at 5 per cent level.

In the societies at Nagercoil, the significant factors influencing default are financial and personal factors. A unit increase in the perception on the above two factors results in an increase in total default amount by 0.5819 and 0.3036 units respectively. In the societies at Thuckalay, a unit increase in the perception on the financial and personal factors results in a significant increase in the default by 0.3981 and 0.2445 units respectively. The analysis of pooled data also reveals that the increase in the above said two factors results in an increase in the default by 0.4087 and 0.2962 units respectively. The change in the included independent variable explains the change in default to the extent of 79.89 per cent.

SERVICE QUALITY OF THE ECTCS

The service quality of ECTCS is measured with the help of SERVQUAL scores. The SERVQUAL score is calculated by the difference between the customers' expectation and perception on the various services offered by the society. Even though the services offered by the society are too many, the present study confines these variables to working hours, time taken for transaction, time taken for processing, quick rectification of mistakes, timely information, availability of staff, consciousness of staff, staff's knowledge, grievances handling, customers relationship, atmosphere, location, network, technology used, accessibility, variety of deposits, variety of loans, variety of rate of interest and value added services (Capoor, 2000).[2]

The members were asked to rate the above said service quality variables at five point scale in two dimensions namely expectation and perception. By expectation, the members were asked to rate with the options highly expected, expected, moderate, not expected and not at all expected whereas by perception, the members were asked to rate with the options highly satisfied, satisfied, moderate, dissatisfied and highly dissatisfied.

The scores of the service quality variables were taken for factor analysis in order to narrate the service quality variables into service quality factors. The factor analysis results in four important factors namely time, interaction, infrastructural facilities and products. The factors, the variables in each factor, their reliability coefficient, Eigen value of the factors are presented in Table 4.36.

The narrated four factors explain the service quality variables to the extent of 68.02 percent. The most important service quality factor was 'time' factor. It consists of five service quality variables with the reliability coefficient of 0.6193. The Eigen value and the per cent of variation of this factor were 3.2409 and 21.32 per cent respectively. The second and third important service quality factors were 'interaction' and 'infrastructural facilities'. The interaction factor consists of five service quality variables with the reliability coefficient of 0.8217. The Eigen value and the per cent of variation of this factor were 2.6241 and 18.67 per cent respectively. The infrastructural facilities factor consists of five service quality variables with the reliability coefficient of 0.6908. The last factor extracted by the factor analysis was 'Product' factor. It consists of four service quality variables with the reliability coefficient of 0.7134. The factor analysis infers that the important service quality factors in the society were 'Time', 'Interaction', 'Infrastructural Facilities' and 'Product' factors.

Table 4.36

Factor Loading of Service Quality Variables

Factors (Eigen Value)	*Variables*	*Factor Loading*	*Reliability Coefficient*	*Per cent of Variation*
Time (3.2409)	Working hours	0.8337	0.6193	21.32
	Time taken for Transaction	0.7402		
	Time taken for Processing	0.6519		
	Quick rectification of mistakes	0.6303		
	Timely information	0.5742		
Interaction (2.6241)	Availability of staff	0.9028	0.8217	18.67
	Consciousness of staff	0.8137		
	Staff knowledge	0.7304		
	Grievances handling	0.6219		
	Customers relationship	0.5401		
Infra-structural Facilities (2.2101)	Atmosphere	0.8433	0.6908	15.39
	Location	0.6928		
	Network	0.6304		
	Technology used	0.5911		
	Accessibility	0.5302		
Products (1.3962)	Variety of deposits	0.9034	0.7134	12.64
	Variety of Loans	0.8243		
	Variety of rate of interest	0.7817		
	Value added services	0.6091		

SERVQUAL Scores of Service Quality Factors of the Societies at Nagercoil

The SERVQUAL score represents the difference between the expectation and perception of the members on the service quality factors. The scores on expectation and perception on the service quality factors were derived from the mean scores of the expectation and perception on the service quality variables in each factor. The means of expectation and perception on the service quality factors, their mean differences and the respective 't' statistics have been computed to exhibit the SERVQUAL score in each factor. The results are shown in Table 4.37.

Table 4.37

Mean of Expectation and Perception of Service Quality in the Societies at Nagercoil

Sl. No.	*Factors in Service Quality*	*Mean Score*		*Mean Difference*	*'t'-Statistics*
		Expectation	*Perception*		
1.	Time	3.9806	3.1143	0.7943	2.0962*
2.	Interaction	3.4517	2.9094	0.5423	1.7102
3.	Infrastructural facilities	2.9663	3.4214	-0.4551	-1.5961
4.	Product	3.2307	2.1826	1.0481	3.3862*

* Significant at 5 per cent level.

The positive mean differences in the service quality factors reveal that the mean of expectation is greater than the mean of perception. The service quality factors with positive mean difference were 'Time', 'Interaction' and 'Product' whereas the significant mean differences were identified in the case of 'Time' and 'Product'. Only in the infrastructural facilities, the SERVQUAL score was negative. It shows that the mean of perception is greater than the mean of expectation but that difference is not statistically significant. This analysis infers that the respondents' perceptions on the various service quality factors of the societies were not up to their level of expectation in the case of societies at Nagercoil.

SERVQUAL Scores of the Societies at Thuckalay

The SERVQUAL scores of the service quality factors have been computed by the difference between the means of expectation and perception on the four service quality factors among the members. The 't' test has been administered to find out the significant differences between the two means. The resulted means of expectation and perception and the respective 't' statistics are presented in Table 4.38.

Table 4.38

Mean of Expectation and Perception of Service Quality in the Societies at Thuckalay

Sl. No.	*Factors in Service Quality*	*Mean Score*		*Mean Difference*	*'t'-Statistics*
		Expectation	*Perception*		
1.	Time	3.6217	2.4517	1.1700	3.0963*
2.	Interaction	3.0962	2.8632	0.2330	0.5139
3.	Infrastructural facilities	2.9791	2.4361	0.5430	0.9786
4.	Product	3.3039	2.0476	1.2563	3.1708*

* Significant at 5 per cent level.

In all four service quality factors, the SERVQUAL scores were positive. It reveals that the mean of expectation was greater than the mean of perception on all service quality factors among the members. The significant mean differences were identified in the case of 'Product' and 'Time' since the respective 't' statistics were significant at five per cent level. The analysis reveals that the perception on the service quality offered by the societies at Thuckalay was not up to the level of expectation among the members.

OVERALL ATTITUDE TOWARDS THE SOCIETIES

The overall attitude of the members towards the societies has been measured. The overall attitude was measured at five point scale with options, highly satisfied, satisfied, moderate, dissatisfied and highly dissatisfied.

Table 4.39 explains the distribution of members on the basis of their overall attitude towards the society. The important levels of attitude among the members were dissatisfied and moderate which constitute 39.01 and 28.01 per cent to the total respectively. The members who were satisfied and highly satisfied with the society constitute only 17.55 per cent to the total. In the societies at Nagercoil and Thuckalay, the levels of overall attitude were dissatisfied and moderate. The analysis infers that the overall attitude towards the society was varying from moderate to dissatisfied among the members.

Table 4.39

Overall Attitude Towards the Societies

Sl. No.	*Overall Attitude*	*Societies at Nagercoil*		*Societies at Thuckalay*		*Total*	
		No. of Members	*Percent-age*	*No. of Members*	*Percent-age*	*No. of Members*	*Percent-age*
1.	Highly Satisfied	22	7.10	17	6.69	39	6.91
2.	Satisfied	36	11.61	24	9.45	60	10.64
3.	Moderate	89	28.71	69	27.17	158	28.01
4.	Dissatisfied	103	33.23	117	46.06	220	39.01
5.	Highly Dissatisfied	60	19.35	27	10.63	87	15.43
	Total	310	100.00	254	100.00	564	100.00

Source: Primary Data.

Association Between the Profile of Members and their Overall Attitude Towards the Society

The profile of the members may have its own influence on the overall attitude towards the society. In order to analyse the association between the profile of members and their overall attitude towards the society, the chi-square analysis was used. The included profile variables were gender, age, level of education, marital status, family size, personal income, family income and personality index. The result of chi-square analysis is shown in Table 4.40.

The significant chi-square x^2 values were identified in a few profile variables namely age, level of education, personal income, family income and personality index since the respective chi-square values were significant at 5 per cent level. It reveals that there is an association between the overall attitude towards the society and the profile of the members especially age, level of education, personal income, family income and personality index.

Table 4.40

Association Between the Profile of Members and their Overall Attitude Towards the Societies

Sl. No.	*Profile Variables*	*Chi-square Value*	*Table Value at 5 per cent level*	*Result*
1.	Gender	8.1714	9.488	Insignificant
2.	Age	53.2962	36.415	Significant
3.	Level of Education	28.9096	26.296	Significant
4.	Occupation	26.0443	31.410	Insignificant
5.	Marital Status	18.1917	21.026	Insignificant
6.	Family Size	23.3908	26.296	Insignificant
7.	Personal Income	31.3086	26.296	Significant
8.	Family Income	36.3914	31.410	Significant
9.	Personality Index	28.0849	26.296	Significant

Impact of Perception on Service Quality Factors on the Overall Attitude Towards Society

The impact of perception of service quality factors on the overall attitude towards the society among the respondents in the societies at Nagercoil and Thuckalay and the pooled data was analysed separately with the help of multiple regression analysis. The scores of the perception on four service quality factors were taken as the score of independent variables. The scores assigned on the overall attitude with options highly satisfied, satisfied, moderate, dissatisfied and highly dissatisfied were 5, 4, 3, 2 and 1 respectively. The fitted regression model is

$$y = a+b_1x_1+b_2x_2+b_3x_3+b_4x_4+e$$

whereas y = Score on overall attitude towards the society

x_1 = Score of the perception on 'Time' factor

x_2 = Score of the perception on 'Interaction' factor

x_3 = Score of the perception on 'Infrastructural facilities' factor

x_4 = Score of the perception on 'Product' factor

b_1, b_2, b_3, b_4 = Regression coefficients of independent variables

a = Intercept and

e = Error term.

Table 4.41

Impact of Perception of Service Quality on Overall Attitude Towards the Society

Sl. No.	*Service Quality Factors*	*Regression Coefficients*		
		Societies at Nagercoil	*Societies at Thuckalay*	*Pooled*
1.	Time	0.2069*	0.2717*	0.2363*
2.	Interaction	0.1437*	0.2173*	0.1609*
3.	Infrastructural Facilities	-.0416	0.0963	0.0737
4.	Product	.1023	0.1708*	0.1122
	Constant	0.5761	0.9891	0.7372
	R^2	0.7237	0.8189	0.8393
	F-Statistics	9.3631*	11.3696*	13.0918*

* Significant at 5 per cent level.

In societies at Nagercoil, the significant influencing perceptions of the service quality factors on the overall attitude among the members were time and interaction. A unit increase in the perception of the above said two factors results in an increase in overall attitude by 0.2069 and 0.1437 units respectively. In the societies at Thuckalay, these variables were the perception on time, interaction and product factor with the regression coefficient of 0.2717, 0.2173 and 0.1708 respectively. The analysis of pooled data revealed that a unit increase in the perception on Time and Interaction results in an increase in overall attitude towards society by 0.2363 and 0.1609 units respectively. The changes in perception on the service quality factors explain the changes in overall attitude among the members to the extent of 83.93 per cent.

MEMBERS' WILLINGNESS TO CONTINUE THEIR MEMBERSHIP

Some members may prefer to continue the membership of the society and some others may want to discontinue the membership because of several reasons. The study on the members' opinion on it is highly imperative to understand and determine the future of the society. In the present study, the opinions were classified into highly liking, liking, disliking and highly disliking. The distribution of respondents on the basis of their opinion is shown in Table 4.42.

Table 4.42

Willingness to Continue as a Member

Sl. No.	*Opinion*	*Societies at Nagercoil*		*Societies at Thuckalay*		*Total*	
		No. of Members	*Percent-age*	*No. of Members*	*Percent-age*	*No. of Members*	*Percent-age*
1.	Highly liking	17	5.48	21	8.27	38	6.74
2.	Liking	76	24.52	69	27.17	145	25.71
3.	Disliking	128	41.29	102	40.16	230	40.78
4.	Highly Disliking	89	28.71	62	24.41	151	26.77
	Total	310	100.00	254	100.00	564	100.00

Source: Primary Data.

In total, a maximum of 40.78 per cent of the total members showed their dislike to continue as members and 26.77 per cent members were highly disliking. The members who were willing to continue as members in the society constitute only 32.45 per cent to the total. In the societies at Nagercoil, the disliking members constitute 41.29 per cent to the total. In societies at Thuckalay, disliking members constitute 40.16 per cent to the total.

REASONS FOR DISLIKING THE MEMBERSHIP

The respondents dislike to be members in the society because of several reasons. The identified reasons in the present study were poor performance of societies, irregularities, strained relationship with staff, poor knowledge among staff, unreliable service, high rate of interest, low loan amount, higher formalities, low interest on deposits, lesser variety of products, requirement of mortgages, higher waiting period for processing, lesser accessibility, poor infrastructural facilities, poor administration, poor modernisation, lesser service quality and lesser transparency. The respondents were asked to narrate the above said eighteen variables at five point scale with options highly agree, agree, moderate, disagree and highly disagree. The scores assigned on the scales were 5, 4, 3, 2 and 1 respectively. The mean scores of the various reasons have been computed to exhibit the importance of the reasons for disliking.

Table 4.43

Mean Score of the Reasons for Disliking to Continue as Members

Sl. No.	*Reasons for Disliking*	*Mean Score*		*'t'-Statistics*
		Societies at Nagercoil	*Societies at Thuckalay*	
1	2	3	4	5
1.	Poor Performance of Societies	2.8917	3.6783	-1.8578
2.	Irregularities	3.0396	2.9176	0.3317
3.	Strained Relationship with Staff	3.4224	2.4562	1.9906*
4.	Poor Knowledge Among Staff	3.6869	3.0143	0.8308
5.	Unreliable Service	3.8182	3.9193	-0.2149
6.	High Rate of Interest	3.9094	3.8182	0.1936
7.	Low Loan Amount	3.9296	3.7671	0.3708
8.	Higher Formalities	2.8181	3.4043	-0.6833

(Contd...)

1	2	3	4	5
9.	Low Rate of Interest on Deposits	2.3036	3.0211	-1.5671
10.	Less Variety of Products	2.8687	3.1719	-0.5024
11.	Requirement of Mortgages	1.9693	2.0676	-0.1391
12.	Higher Waiting Period for Processing	2.7131	2.3434	0.7242
13.	Lesser Accessibility	2.8087	2.9908	-0.2963
14.	Poor Infrastructural Facilities	1.8684	2.3046	-0.5781
15.	Poor Administration	2.4543	3.8181	-2.7962*
16.	Poor Modernisation	2.4042	3.6261	-2.3391*
17.	Less Service Quality	3.6061	2.7173	2.1976*
18.	Less Transparency	2.9798	3.0962	-0.2073

* Significant at 5 per cent level.

Table 4.43 explains the mean scores of various reasons for disliking the membership among the members in the societies at Nagercoil and Thuckalay. The highly viewed reasons for dislike among the members in societies at Nagercoil were low loan amount, high rate of interest and unreliable service since the respective mean scores were 3.9296, 3.9094 and 3.8182 respectively. In societies at Thuckalay, these were unreliable service, high rate of interest and poor administration since the respective mean scores were 3.9193, 3.8182 and 3.8181. Regarding the perception on the reasons for dislike, the significant differences among the members in two groups of societies were identified in the perception on the reasons such as relationship with staff, poor administration, poor modernisation and lesser service quality since the respective 't-statistics' were significant at five per cent level.

Narration of the Reasons for Disliking into Factors

The included reasons for unwilling to continue as the member in the society were narrated with the help of factor analysis. The scores on various reasons for reluctance were taken into account for the analysis. The factor analysis results in four important factors leading to unwillingness among the members. These were service quality, office formalities, product and finance factor. The resulted factors, their Eigen value, per cent of variation, variables in each factor and its reliability coefficient are presented in Table 4.44.

Table 4.44

Important Factors for Disliking among the Members

Factors (Eigen Value)	*R Reasons for Disliking*	*Factor Loading*	*Reliability Coefficient*	*Per cent of Variation*
Service Quality (3.8917)	Less Service Quality	0.9024	0.8163	23.98
	Less Transparency	0.8217		
	Poor Performance	0.7609		
	Strained Relationship with Staff	0.7126		
	Unreliable Service	0.6579		
	Poor Knowledge Among the Staffs	0.5934		
Office Formalities (3.0691)	Irregularities	0.8919	0.7308	20.04
	Higher Formalities	0.7608		
	Lesser Accessibility	0.7142		
	Higher Waiting Period for Processing	0.6336		
	Non-accessibility	0.6063		
Product (2.0818)	Lesser Variety of Products	0.8702	0.6933	14.36
	Poor Modernisation	0.7119		
	Poor Infrastructural Facilities	0.6304		
	Requirement of Mortgages	0.5921		
Finance (1.4963)	Low Loan Amount	0.9232	0.8398	12.17
	Higher Rate of Interest on Loans	0.8317		
	Low Rate of Interest on Deposits	0.8143		

The narrated four factors explain the reasons for unwillingness to the extent of 70.55 per cent. The most important factor was 'service quality factor' which consists of six reasons with the reliability coefficient of 0.8163. The Eigen value and the per cent of variation of the factor were 3.8917 and 23.98 per cent respectively. The second important factor was the 'office formalities' which consists of five reasons with the reliability coefficient of 0.7308. The Eigen value and the per cent of variation of this factor were 3.0691 and 20.04 per cent respectively. The next two important factors were product and finance factors consisting of four and three reasons respectively.

PROBLEMS ENCOUNTERED BY THE MEMBERS

The members experience so many problems with the society while they are applying for loans. In order to rectify the problems encountered by the members the present study has made an attempt to analyse the problems faced by the members. The problems are identified with the help of some reviews. (Taori, 2005[3] and NSSO, 2002).[4]

Even though, the problems are too many, the present study confined these problems to procedural formalities, limited loan amount, hypothecation, higher rate of interest, poor response, delay in sanctioning loan, limited working hours, rigidity, lesser transparency, staff's behaviour, time taken to process the loan application, lack of communication, poor knowledge among members of staff, unreliability on the service and poor service quality. The members were asked to rate the above said 15 problems at five point scale with options highly true, true, moderate, not true and not at all true. The marks assigned on these scales were 5, 4, 3, 2 and 1 respectively. The mean score of each problem has been calculated to exhibit the importance of the problems.

Table 4.45

Problems Encountered by the Members

Sl. No.	*Problems*	*Mean Score*		*'t'-Statistics*
		Societies at Nagercoil	*Societies at Thuckalay*	
1.	Procedural formalities	3.8186	3.9171	-0.2362
2.	Limited Loan	3.4641	3.3068	0.1171
3.	Hypothecation	2.7081	3.4121	-1.3309
4.	Higher Rate of Interest	3.8917	2.5712	2.2144*
5.	Poor Response	2.8084	2.1176	1.4561
6.	Delay in Sanctioning of Loan	2.9192	2.8081	0.3032
7.	Limited Working hours	2.4647	3.5069	-2.1708*
8.	Rigidity	3.3396	3.7678	-0.3391
9.	Lesser Transparency	2.5181	3.1142	-0.7089
10.	Staff Behaviour	3.2069	3.4549	-0.3039
11.	Time taken to process the Loan application	3.8093	3.1714	0.4546
12.	Lack of Communication	2.7183	3.5671	-1.9968*
13.	Poor Knowledge among members of Staff	3.4246	3.8643	-0.7361
14.	Unreliability on the Service	2.8081	3.9194	-2.1718*
15.	Poor Service Quality	3.8984	3.3086	0.9682

* Significant at 5 per cent level.

Table 4.45 explains the importance of the problems among the members with their mean scores. The highly viewed problems among the members in the societies at Nagercoil were poor service quality, higher rate of interest and procedural formalities since the respective mean scores were 3.8984, 3.8917 and 3.8186. In the societies at Thuckalay, these were unreliability on the service, procedural formalities and poor knowledge among the staff since the respective mean scores were 3.9194, 3.9171 and 3.8643. Regarding the problem perception, the significant differences among the members in two groups of societies have been identified in the perception on higher rate of interest, limited working hours, lack of communication and unreliability on the service since the respective 't' statistics were significant at five per cent level.

Important Problems Encountered by the Members

The study covers fifteen problems. Even though all the problems are equally important, there is a necessity to narrate these problems into meaningful important factors (problems) for further analysis. For that purpose, the factor analysis has been administered. The scores of the fifteen problems among the members were taken into account. The factor analysis results in four important (problems) factors namely office formalities, service quality, members of staff and product oriented problems. The number of problems in each factor, their reliability coefficient, the Eigen of the factor and their per cent of variation explained are shown in Table 4.46.

The narrated four important factors explain the problems encountered by the members to the extent of 76.11 per cent. The most important factor identified by the factor analysis was the 'official formalities'. It consists of five problems with the reliability coefficient of 0.7331. The Eigen value and the per cent of variation explained by this factor were 3.9698 and 21.89 per cent respectively. The second important factor was 'service quality' factor with the Eigen value and per cent of variation of 3.0611 and 20.02 per cent respectively. It consists of four problems with the reliability coefficient of 0.8415. The last two important factors were 'staff' and 'product' with the Eigen values of 2.4503 and 1.8691 respectively. The 'staff' factor consists of four problems with the reliability coefficient of 0.8661 whereas the 'product' factor consists of two problems with the reliability of 0.7174. The important problems faced by the members, narrated by factor analysis were office formalities, service quality, staff and product.

Table 4.46

Factor Loading of the Problems

Factors (Eigen Value)	*Problems*	*Factor Loading*	*Reliability Coefficient*	*Per cent of Variation*
Office Formalities (3.9698)	Procedural formalities	0.8981	0.7331	21.89
	Hypothecation	0.8063		
	Rigidity	0.7229		
	Time taken to process loan application	0.6864		
	Limited working hours	0.6164		
Service Quality (3.0611)	Poor Service Quality	0.9183	0.8415	20.02
	Poor Receptiveness	0.8998		
	Delay in Sanctioning of Loan	0.8104		
	Lesser Transparency	0.7565		
Staff (2.4503)	Staff behaviour	0.8786	0.8661	18.71
	Lack of Communication	0.8017		
	Unreliability on the Service	0.7331		
Product (1.8691)	Poor Knowledge among the members of staff	0.8446	0.7174	15.49
	Limited Loam Amount	0.8081		
	Higher Rate of Interest	0.6292		

Association Between the Profile of Respondents and their Problem Perception

The problem perception among the members was analysed with their perception on the four important factors namely office formalities, service quality, staffs and product. The scores of the above said four factors were drawn from the mean scores of the problems in each factor. Since the profile of the members may have its own impact on the problem perception of the members, the study has made an attempt to analyse the association between the profile variables and their problem perception. The included profile variables were gender, age, level of education, occupation, marital status, family size, personal income, family income and personality index. The one way analysis of variance was administered to find out such association. The resulted 'F' statistics are presented in Table 4.47.

Table 4.47

Association Between Profile of Members and their Perception on Problems

Sl. No.	*Profile*	*F-Statistics*			
		Office Formalities	*Service Quality*	*Staff*	*Product*
1.	Gender	2.9811	3.9671*	2.4086	1.9182
2.	Age	2.0696	1.8081	2.4111*	2.6384*
3.	Level of Education	2.6187*	1.9192	2.5096*	2.4108*
4.	Occupation	2.0681	1.8683	1.7023	2.8386*
5.	Marital Status	2.1132	1.7182	1.0896	2.1171
6.	Family Size	2.0896	1.9787	2.1142	2.3671
7.	Personal Income	3.1108*	2.9696*	2.0811	2.2632
8.	Family Income	3.4317*	2.7208*	2.9601*	3.1717*
9.	Personality Index	2.5082*	3.0814*	2.7086*	3.2021*

* Significant at 5 per cent level.

Regarding the perception on office formalities, the significant associating profile variables were level of education, personal income, family income and personality index since the respective 'F' statistics were significant at five per cent level. By the perception on the service quality problem, the significant differences among the members were identified when they were classified on the basis of gender, personal income, family income and personality index. The significantly associating profile variables with the problem perception on the staff and related problems were age, level of education, family income and personality index since the respective 'F' statistics were significant at five per cent level. By the perception on the 'product' factor, the significantly associating profile variables were age, level of education, occupation, family income and personality index since the respective 'F' statistics were significant at five per cent level.

Impact of Problem Perception on the Overall Attitude Towards the Society

The problem perception among the members has its own impact on the overall attitude towards the society. In order to analyse the impact of perception of important problems on the overall attitude towards the society, the multiple regression analysis has been administered. The scores of problem perception on office formalities, service quality, staff and product were taken as the scores of independent variables. The score on overall attitude towards the society was treated as the score of the dependent variable. The fitted regression model is

$$y = a+b_1x_1+b_2x_2+b_3x_3+b_4x_4+e$$

whereas y = Score on overall attitude towards the society

x_1 = Score of the problem perception on office formalities

x_2 = Score of the problem perception on service quality

x_3 = Score of the problem perception on staff

x_4 = Score of the problem perception on product

b_1, b_2, b_3, b_4 = Regression coefficients of independent variables

a = Intercept and

e = Error term.

The regression analysis was carried out in case of the societies at Nagercoil and Thuckalay and also for pooled data. The resulted regression coefficients are presented in Table 4.48.

Table 4.48

Impact of Problem Perception on Overall Attitude Towards Society

Sl. No.	*Problems (Factors)*	*Regression Coefficients*		
		Societies at Nagercoil	*Societies at Thuckalay*	*Pooled*
1.	Office Formalities	.0962	-0.1781*	-0.1033
2.	Service Quality	-0.3147*	-0.2402*	-0.2606*
3.	Staff	-0.1123	0.1081	0.0731
4.	Product	-0.1908*	-0.1334*	-0.1536*
	Constant	-0.2317	-0.7867	-0.5859
	R^2	0.7239	0.7011	0.8681
	F-Statistics	8.6824*	8.4384*	11.9172*

* Significant at 5 per cent level.

The significant influencing problem perceptions on the overall attitude towards the society among the members in the societies at Nagercoil, were problem perceptions on service quality and product since the respective regression coefficients were –0.3147 and –0.1908. In the societies at Thuckalay, these variables were the problem perception on office formalities, service quality and product. The analysis of pooled data revealed that a unit increase in the problem perceptions on service quality and product results in a decrease in overall attitude towards the society by 0.2606 and 0.1536 units respectively. The changes in the problem perception explain the changes in overall attitude towards the society to the extent of 86.81 per cent.

SUGGESTIONS FOR THE IMPROVEMENT OF THE SOCIETIES

The improvement of the functioning and performance of the societies requires various policy implications. The present study has made an attempt to reveal the various remedial measures to improve the functioning of the societies. The improvement measures are drawn from the reviews

(Satyanarayana, 1999[5]; Amin, 2004[6] and Gupta, 2003[7]) and the experts in the field. The identified improvement measures in the present study are appointment of knowledgeable members of staff, wider range of products, training to the staff, increase in the loan amount, various rates of interest, increase in working hours, flexibility, strict in collection of overdue, follow up actions, speedy processing, periodical analysis, regularity in payment of dividend, proper communication and improvement in reliability. The members were asked to rate the above said 14 measures at five point scale with options highly important, important, moderate, not important, and not at all important. The scores assigned on these scales were 5, 4, 3, 2 and 1 respectively. The mean scores on the measures for improvement were calculated to identify the measures which requires immediate attention. The 't' test has been used to analyse the significant differences among the members in two groups of societies regarding their perception on the importance given to these variables. The results are shown in Table 4.49.

Table 4.49

Measures for the Improvement of the Societies

Sl. No.	*Measures*	*Mean Score*		*'t'-Statistics*
		Societies at Nagercoil	*Societies at Thuckalay*	
1	2	3	4	5
1.	Appoint knowledgeable employed	3.1783	3.8543	-1.4517
2.	Wider Range of Products	3.8821	2.7617	2.0276*
3.	Training to the Staff	3.3081	3.6042	-0.5082
4.	Increase the Loan Amount	3.7011	3.9676	-0.4119
5.	Various Rates of Interest	2.7142	3.8231	-2.1783*
6.	Increase in Working hours	2.4562	2.9697	-0.6381
7.	Flexibility	3.1148	2.4508	0.8814
8.	Strict in Collection of Overdue	3.3324	3.7604	-0.5067

(Contd...)

1	2	3	4	5
9.	Follow up Actions	2.9697	3.8183	-2.0381*
10.	Speedy Processing	3.4571	3.6267	-0.3637
11.	Periodical Analysis	2.9092	3.0891	-0.0918
12.	Regularity in Payment of Dividend	3.8182	3.1143	0.9693
13.	Proper Communication	2.7147	2.5607	0.3031
14.	Improvement in Reliability	3.8617	3.4042	0.7243

* Significant at 5 per cent level.

The important measures identified by the members in the societies at Nagercoil were wider range of products, improvement in reliability and regularity in payment of dividend since the respective mean scores were 3.8821, 3.8617 and 3.8182 respectively. In the societies at Thuckalay, these were increase in loan amount, appointment of knowledgeable members of staff and various rates of interest since the respective mean scores were 3.9676, 3.8543 and 3.8231. Regarding the importance given on the improvement measures, the significant differences among the members in two groups of societies have been identified in the perception on various rates of interest, wider range of products and follow up actions since the respective 't' statistics were significant at five per cent level.

Important Improvement Factors

In order to identify the important improvement factors, the scores on various improvement measures have been taken into account for factor analysis. The factor analysis results in three important improvement measures namely office work, staff and product. The Eigen value, per cent of variation explained by the factor, variables in each factor and its reliability coefficients are shown in Table 4.50.

Table 4.50

Factor Loading of the Suggestions for the Improvement of the Society

Factors (Eigen Value)	*Suggestions*	*Factor Loading*	*Reliability Coefficient*	*Per cent of Variation*
Office Work (3.1172)	Increase in Working hours	0.9234	0.7314	23.48
	Strict in Collection of Overdue	0.7827		
	Periodical Analysis	0.7331		
	Regularity in Payment of Dividend	0.6496		
	Speedy Processing	0.6082		
	Follow up Actions	0.5549		
Staff (2.4671)	Training to the Staffs	0.8784	0.7192	20.91
	Proper Communication	0.8029		
	Improvement in Reliability	0.7192		
	Appoint Knowledgeable Members of Staff	0.6406		
Product (1.9303)	Wider Range of Product	0.9091	0.7508	17.33
	Variety of Rate of Interest Flexibility	0.8134 0.7096		
	Increase in Loan Amount	0.6237		

The important improvement factors explain the measures for improvement of the societies to the extent of 61.72 per cent. The primary factor was 'office work' which consists of six measures with the reliability coefficient of 0.7314. The Eigen value and the per cent of variation explained by the factor were 3.1172 and 23.48 per cent respectively. The second important factor 'Staff' consists of four variables with the reliability coefficient of 0.7192. The Eigen value and the per cent of variation by the factor were 2.4671 and 20.91 per cent respectively. The last factor identified by the factor analysis was the 'Product' factor. It consists of four important measures with the reliability coefficient of 1.9303. The most important measures in each factor are increase in working hours, training to the staff and wider range of products since the factor loadings were higher in the respective factors. The factor analysis results in three important improvement factors for the enrichment of the performance of the societies.

Association Between the Profile of the Members and their Opinion on Improvement Factors

The identified improved factors were office work, staff and product. The scores on these factors were calculated from the scores of the improvement measures in each factor. The mean scores of the improvement measures were treated as the scores of the improvement factors. The opinion on the improvement factors may vary from person to person. In general, the profile of respondents play a vital role in the opinion on the improvement factors. In order to analyse the association between the profile of the members and their opinion on the improvement factors, the one way analysis has been administered. The resulted 'F' statistics are shown in Table 4.51.

Table 4.51

Association Between the Profile of Members and their View on Suggestions

Sl. No.	*Profile Variables*	*'F' - Statistics*		
		Office Work	*Staff*	*Product*
1.	Gender	2.9168	2.0811	3.9114*
2.	Age	2.0814	1.9896	2.0234
3.	Level of Education	2.7619*	2.5083*	3.1718*
4.	Occupation	1.8381	1.0817	2.0961
5.	Marital Status	2.3006	1.9182	2.2634
6.	Family Size	1.7917	2.0863	2.3011
7.	Personal Income	2.7082*	3.1173*	3.0846*
8.	Family Income	3.0896*	2.7081*	2.4643*
9.	Personality Index	3.2114*	2.6708*	2.6504*

* Significant at 5 per cent level.

Regarding the opinion on the office work factor, the significantly associating profile variables were level of education, personal income, family income and personality index since the respective 'F' statistics were significant at 5 per cent level. Regarding the 'staff' factor, the significant differences among the members were identified when they were classified on the basis of level of education, personal income, family income and personality index. In the case of 'product' factor, the significantly associating profile variables were gender, level of education, personal income, family income and personality index since the respective 'F' statistics were significant at five per cent level. Among the profile variables, the important profile variables associate with the opinion on the important factors were level of education, personal income, family income and personality index.

SUMMARY

The analysis of the members attitude and problems encountered by the members revealed that they were not satisfied with the performance of the ECTCS The factor analysis of the suggestions for the improvement of the societies resulted in three factors namely office work, staff and product. The second important factor was staff of ECTCS So in the next chapter an attempt has been made to analyse the profile of the employees of E.C.T.C.S, their attitude and problems to have a clear vision regarding the performance and prospects of ECTCS

REFERENCES

1. Jain, P.K., "Marketing Management of Cooperative Sector", *Tamil Nadu Journal of Co-operation*, 91(2), March 2000, p. 59.

2. Jagadish Capoor, "Urban Cooperative Banks: Problems and Prospects", *Reserve Bank of India Bulletin*, July 2000, pp. 773-780.

3. Taori, "An Analytical View on Urban Cooperative Banks", *The Cooperatives*, 42(10), April 2005, pp. 411-415.

4. NSSO, "An Alternative Model for Salary Earners' Cooperative Credit Societies and Banks", *Urban Credit*, 24(1), March 2002, pp. 15-19.

5. Satyanarayana, G.S., "Challenges Before Scheduled and Large UCBs in the New Millennium", *Urban Credit*, 21(4), 1999, pp. 27-29.

6. Amin, G.H., "Need for Greater Transparency in Urban Cooperative Banks", *The Cooperator*, 41(9), 2004, pp. 3-7.
7. Gupta, R.R., "An Appraisal of the Working of Scheduled UCBs in India — Problems and Prospects", *The Cooperator*, 5(1), February 2003, p. 348.

5

EMPLOYEES ATTITUDE TOWARDS ECTCS

INTRODUCTION

The employees of ECTCS have their own experiences with the customers, officers and co-workers related to the society. Since the experience provides more knowledge than any other thing, the present study has made an attempt to analyse the attitude, problems and suggestions of the employees on functions of ECTCS.

PROFILE OF THE EMPLOYEES

In order to provide the background information about the employees, the profile of the employees have been included in the present study. The included profile variables are gender, age, level of education, years of experience, monthly income, family income and banking orientation.

Gender of the Employees

Since the gender of the employee has its own impact on the exposure of attitudes on various aspects in the society, it is included as one of the profile variables. In general, the male employees are having better exposure on all dimensions towards the societies. The gender of the employees in the two groups of societies are presented in Table 5.1.

Table 5.1

Gender of the Employees

Sl. No.	*Gender*	*Societies at Nagercoil*		*Societies at Thuckalay*		*Total*	
		No. of Employees	*Percent-age*	*No. of Employees*	*Percent-age*	*No. of Employees*	*Percent-age*
1.	Male	35	76.09	21	80.77	56	77.78
2.	Female	11	23.91	5	19.23	16	22.22
	Total	46	100.00	26	100.00	72	100.00

Source: Primary Data.

In total, 77.78 per cent of the employees were males whereas the remaining 22.22 per cent of the employees were females. In the societies at Nagercoil, the male employees selected for the present study constitute 76.09 per cent whereas in the societies at Thuckalay, they constitute 80.77 per cent to the total. The female employees selected for the present study in the societies at Nagercoil constitute 23.91 per cent to the total whereas in the societies at Thuckalay they were 19.23 per cent.

Age of the Employees

The age of the employees indicates their level of maturity and exposure of various aspects related to the ECTCS. So that, it is included as one of the profile variables. In general, the aged employees have more patience to expose their experience in the societies than the youngsters. The age of the employees was confined to less than 30 years, 30 to 40 years, 41 to 50 years, and above 50 years. The distribution of employees according to their age is shown in Table 5.2.

Table 5.2

Age of the Employees

Sl. No.	*Age*	*Societies at Nagercoil*		*Societies at Thuckalay*		*Total*	
		No. of Employees	*Percent-age*	*No. of Employees*	*Percent-age*	*No. of Employees*	*Percent-age*
1.	Less than 30	3	6.52	1	3.85	4	5.56
2.	30-40	11	23.91	8	30.77	19	26.39
3.	41-50	16	34.78	12	46.15	28	38.89
4.	Above 50	16	34.78	5	19.23	21	29.17
	Total	46	100.00	26	100.00	72	100.00

Source: Primary Data.

The common age groups of the employees were 41 to 50 years and above 50 years which constitute 38.89 and 29.17 per cent to the total respectively. In the societies at Nagercoil, these two were 41 to 50 years and above 50 years which constitute 34.78 per cent each to the total of 46 employees. In societies at Thuckalay, these two groups were 41 to 50 years and 30-40 years which constitute 46.15 and 30.77 per cent to the total of 26 employees respectively.

Level of Education of the Employees

Since the level of education among the employees provides more knowledge and analytical power to the employees, it is included as one of the profile variables. The educated employees have wide knowledge and exposure on various aspects of ECTCS. The level of education in the present study was confined to school education, diploma education, graduation, post-graduation and others. The distribution of employees according to their level of education is illustrated in Table 5.3.

Table 5.3

Level of Education of the Employees

Sl. No.	*Level of Education*	*Societies at Nagercoil*		*Societies at Thuckalay*		*Total*	
		No. of Employees	*Percentage*	*No. of Employees*	*Percentage*	*No. of Employees*	*Percentage*
1.	School education	4	8.70	3	11.54	7	9.72
2.	Diploma education	6	13.04	4	15.38	10	13.89
3.	Graduation	23	50.00	11	42.31	34	47.22
4.	Post-graduation	7	15.22	4	15.38	11	15.28
5.	Others	6	13.04	4	15.38	10	13.89
	Total	46	100.00	26	100.00	72	100.00

Source: Primary Data.

The common levels of education among the employees are graduation and post-graduation which constitute 47.22 and 15.28 per cent to the total respectively. The number of employees who have an education level of diploma education and school education constitute 13.89 and 9.72 per cent to the total respectively. The most important level of education among the employees of the societies at Nagercoil was graduation which constitutes 50.00 per cent to the total whereas in the societies at Thuckalay, the common level was graduation which constitutes 42.31 per cent to the total.

Years of Experience

The years of experience among the employees represent the number of years they have worked in the societies. Since the years of experience reveal the level of awareness and knowledge on the various functioning of societies, it is included as a profile variable in the present study. The levels of experience were confined to less than 5 years, 5 to 10 years, 11 to 15 years, 16 to 20 years and above 20 years. The distribution of employees according to their years of experience is exhibited in Table 5.4.

Table 5.4

Years of Experience of the Employees

Sl. No.	Years of Experience	Societies at Nagercoil		Societies at Thuckalay		Total	
		No. of Employees	Percentage	No. of Employees	Percentage	No. of Employees	Percentage
1.	Less than 5 years	7	15.22	5	19.23	12	16.67
2.	5 – 10	12	26.09	7	26.92	19	26.39
3.	11 – 15	13	28.26	10	38.46	23	31.94
4.	16 – 20	11	23.91	2	7.69	13	18.06
5.	Above 20 years	3	6.52	2	7.69	5	6.94
	Total	46	100.00	26	100.00	72	100.00

Source: Primary Data.

The most common years of experience among the employees in the present study were 11 to 15 years and 5 to 10 years which constitute 31.94 and 26.39 per cent to the total respectively. In the societies at Nagercoil, the common years of experience was 11 to 15 years, which constitutes 28.26 per cent to the total. In the case of societies at Thuckalay, the common years of experience were 11 to 15 and 5 to 10 years respectively which constitute 38.46 and 26.92 per cent to the total respectively.

Monthly Income

The income of the employees represents the monthly income received by the employees from the society as their salary. Since, the monthly income shows the standard of living of the employees, it is included as one of the profile variables. The monthly income may have its own impact on the knowledge and awareness on the aspects in the society. The monthly income was confined to less than Rs. 2,000; Rs. 2,000-4,000; Rs. 4,001-6,000; Rs. 6,001-8,000 and above Rs. 8,000 in the present study. The distribution of employees on the basis of their monthly income is shown in Table 5.5.

Table 5.5

Monthly Income of the Employees

Sl. No.	Monthly Income (Rs.)	Societies at Nagercoil		Societies at Thuckalay		Total	
		No. of Employees	Percentage	No. of Employees	Percentage	No. of Employees	Percentage
1.	Less than 2000	4	8.70	2	7.69	6	8.33
2.	2000 – 4000	11	23.91	10	38.46	21	29.17
3.	4001 – 6000	10	21.74	8	30.77	18	25.00
4.	6001 – 8,000	8	17.39	2	7.69	10	13.89
5.	Above 8,000	13	28.26	4	15.38	17	23.61
	Total	46	100.00	26	100.00	72	100.00

Source: Primary Data.

The important categories of monthly income among the employees were Rs. 2,000 to 4,000 and Rs. 4,001 to 6,000 which constitute 29.17 and 25.00 per cent to the total respectively. The employees who earn a monthly income of less than Rs. 2000 constitute 8.33 per cent to the total. In the societies at Nagercoil, the common monthly income of the employees were above Rs. 8,000 and Rs. 2000 to 4000 which constitute 28.26 and 23.91 per cent to its total of 46 employees. In societies at Thuckalay, these two were Rs. 2000 to 4000 and Rs. 4001 to 6000 which constitute 38.46 and 30.77 per cent to the total respectively.

Banking Orientation

The banking orientation indicates the level of knowledge and involvement on the banking activities of the societies. Since the banking orientation may exhibit more idea on the functioning of the society, it is included as one of the profile variables of the employees. The banking orientation among the employees has been measured with the help of some related statements. The employees were asked to rate the statements at five point scale.

From the score obtained, the employees' banking orientation has been calculated. In the present study, the level of banking orientation was classified into excellent, good, moderate, poor and very poor. The banking orientation among the employees is exhibited in Table 5.6.

Table 5.6

Banking Orientation of the Employees

Sl. No.	*Banking Orientation*	*Societies at Nagercoil*		*Societies at Thuckalay*		*Total*	
		No. of Employees	*Percentage*	*No. of Employees*	*Percentage*	*No. of Employees*	*Percentage*
1.	Excellent	2	4.35	2	7.69	4	5.56
2.	Good	7	15.22	4	15.38	11	15.28
3.	Moderate	16	34.78	7	26.92	23	31.94
4.	Poor	15	32.61	8	30.77	23	31.94
5.	Very poor	6	13.04	5	19.23	11	15.28
	Total	46	100.00	26	100.00	72	100.00

Source: Primary Data.

In total, 63.88 per cent of the employees were moderate (31.94%) and poor)31.94%) in their banking orientation whereas only 20.84 per cent of the employees were good (15.28%) and excellent (5.56%) in this aspect. In the societies at Nagercoil, the common levels of banking orientation among the employees were moderate and poor which constitute 34.78 and 32.61 per cent to the total of 46 employees respectively. In the societies at Thuckalay, these two levels were poor and moderate which constitute 30.77 and 26.92 per cent to the total of 26 employees respectively.

VARIABLES INFLUENCING THE SANCTION OF LOAN

The loans applied by the members are appraised and processed by the officials at different dimensions. In the present study, the variables considered for sanction of loans are identified with the help of some reviews (Elumalai, 1999[1]; Shah and Deepak, 1997[2]; and Jugale and Pail, 1998[3]).

The identified variables are income certificate, nature of loans, integrity of borrowers, opinion of others, guarantor certificate, loan amount, amount of deposits by members, officers' influence, known persons, past personal history of borrowers, rate of interest, mortgages, credit worthiness, repayment period and political influence. The employees were asked to rate the above said fifteen variables at five point scale with options highly considered to not at all considered. The scores assigned on these options were from 5 marks to 1 mark.

The mean score of each variable was computed to exhibit the relative importance of the variables on sanctioning the loan. The 't' test was applied to find out the significant differences between the employees in two groups of societies regarding their perception on the variables considered for the sanction of loan. The resulted mean scores of the variables and their respective 't' statistics are shown in Table 5.7.

The highly considered variables to sanction the loan to the employees of the societies at Nagercoil were income certificate, guarantor certificate and credit worthiness since its respective mean scores were 3.8217, 3.7302 and 3.4542 whereas the least considered variables were opinion of others, past personal history of the borrowers and nature of loan since their mean scores were 2.2624, 2.3039 and 2.4083 respectively.

Among the employees of the societies at Thuckalay, the highly considered variables to sanction loans were loan amount, repayment period and mortgages since the mean scores were 3.8689, 3.3303 and 3.2146 respectively whereas the least considered variables were past personal history of the borrowers, known persons and amount of deposits by the members since the respective mean scores were 2.1703, 2.4506 and 2.4576. Regarding the perception on the variables considered to sanction the loan, the significant differences among the employees in two groups of societies were identified in case of perception on income certificate, guarantor certificate and loan amount since the respective 't' statistics were significant at five per cent level.

Table 5.7

Variables Influencing the Sanction of Loan to Staff

Sl. No.	Variables	Mean Score in		't'-Statistics
		Societies at Nagercoil	Societies at Thuckalay	
1.	Income certificate	3.8217	3.0679	2.0234*
2.	Nature of loan	2.4083	2.9117	-1.3311
3.	Integrity of borrowers	3.0943	3.2063	-0.4069
4.	Opinion of others	2.2624	2.8086	-0.67821
5.	Guarantor certificate	3.7302	2.5172	2.5183*
6.	Loan amount	2.8081	3.8689	-2.2671*
7.	Amount of deposits by members	2.3411	2.4576	-0.1192
8.	Officers influence	2.8089	3.1179	-0.4246
9.	Known persons	2.6143	2.4506	0.3031
10.	Past personal history of borrowers	2.3039	2.1703	0.2503
11.	Rate of interest	2.7172	2.5056	0.3117
12.	Mortgages	2.8081	3.2146	-0.5191
13.	Credit worthiness	3.4542	3.0867	0.5028
14.	Repayment period	3.0962	3.3303	-0.4429
15.	Political influence	2.7686	2.6331	0.1782

* Significant at five per cent level.

Factors Considered to Sanction the Loan

The important factors considered to sanction the loan among the employees were found out with the help of factor analysis. The factor analysis was used to narrate the identified fifteen variables considered to sanction the loan for further analysis. The scores of the fifteen variables have been included for the factor analysis. The factor analysis results in four important factors namely security, loan, personal and social factors. Factor loading, its reliability coefficient and per cent of variation are presented in Table 5.8.

Table 5.8

Factor Loading of the Variables Considered to Sanction the Loan

Factors (Eigen value)	*Variables*	*Factor loading*	*Reliability coefficient*	*Per cent of variation*
Security (3.8602)	Income certificate	0.8308	0.8134	22.46
	Credit worthiness	0.7962		
	Guarantor certificate	0.7103		
	Mortgages	0.6341		
Loan (2.4517)	Nature of loan	0.9234	0.8396	20.65
	Loan amount	0.8086		
	Rate of interest	0.7131		
	Payment period	0.6908		
Personal (1.8121)	Integrity of borrowers	0.8221	0.7491	17.36
	Amount of deposits by members	0.7086		
	Past history	0.6553		
Social (1.3396)	Opinion of others	0.8414	0.7565	15.37
	Officers influence	0.7506		
	Known persons	0.6817		
	Political influence	0.6231		

The included fifteen variables explain the four factors considered to sanction the loan to the extent of 75.84 per cent. The most important factor was 'security' factor which consists of four variables with the reliability coefficient of 0.8134. The Eigen value and the per cent of variation explained by this factor were 3.8602 and 22.46 per cent respectively. The second important factor was 'Loan' factor which consists of four variables with the reliability coefficient of 0.8396. The Eigen value and the per cent of variation of this factor were 2.4517 and 20.65 per cent respectively. The third and fourth important factors were personal and social factors with the Eigen values of 1.8121 and 1.3396 respectively. The personal factor consists of three variables with the reliability coefficient of 0.7491 whereas the social factor consists of four variables with the reliability coefficient of 0.7565. The most important variables in the security and loan factors were income certificate and loan amount respectively.

Time Taken to Process the Loan Application

The time taken to process the application of loans is a major problem in the ECTCS. After Globalisation, the commercial banks are competing with each other regarding the processing time to evaluate the loan applications. The new private sector banks never like to take more than 24 hours to process the loan applications. The other commercial banks are trying to cope with this. But the co-operative banks and the ECTCS take more time to process the loan applications. This is also identified as a major drawback of the societies by the members. Hence, an attempt has been made to reveal the average time taken by the societies to process the loan applications. The 'time taken' was confined to less than 15 days, 15 to 30 days, 31 to 45 days, 46 to 60 days and more than 60 days. The distribution of employees according to their view on time taken to process the loan applications is shown in Table 5.9.

Table 5.9

Time Taken to Process the Loan Applications

Sl. No.	*Time Taken*	*Societies at Nagercoil*		*Societies at Thuckalay*		*Total*	
		No. of Employees	*Percentage*	*No. of Employees*	*Percentage*	*No. of Employees*	*Percentage*
1.	Less than 15 days	8	17.39	3	11.54	11	15.28
2.	15 – 30 days	9	19.57	5	19.23	14	19.44
3.	31 – 45 days	12	26.09	7	26.92	19	26.39
4.	46 – 60 days	9	19.57	6	23.08	15	20.83
5.	More than 60 days	8	17.39	5	19.23	13	18.06
	Total	46	100.00	26	100.00	72	100.00

Source: Primary Data.

The first two categories of time taken to process the loan applications were 31 to 45 days and 46 to 60 days which constitute 26.39 and 20.83 per cent to the total respectively. The number of staff with a view of only less than 15 days to process the loan applications constitutes only 15.28 per cent to the total. In societies at Nagercoil, the time taken as per the view of the staff was 31 to 45 days which constitutes 26.09 per cent of the total staff of the societies. In societies at Thuckalay, this was also 31 to 45 days as per the views of 26.92 per cent of the staff.

Reasons for Delay in Sanctioning the Loan

Compared to the commercial banks, the societies usually take more time to sanction the loan. In order to avoid these delays in future, it is imperative to analyse the reasons for such delay. Even though, the reasons for it are too many, the present study confined these reasons to only eleven. These eleven reasons are identified with the help of reviews (Lal and Lavania, 1986;[4] Singh *et al.*, 1989;[5] and Palanisamy *et al.*, 1991[6]). The employees were asked to rate the above said eleven reasons at five point scale with options highly agree, agree, moderate, disagree and highly disagree. The scores assigned on the scales were 5, 4, 3, 2 and 1 respectively. The mean scores of the reasons have been calculated to exhibit their importance.

Table 5.10

Reasons for Delay in Sanctioning the Loan

Sl. No.	*Reasons*	*Mean Score*		*'t'-Statistics*
		Societies at Nagercoil	*Societies at Thuckalay*	
1.	Partially filled application	3.4508	3.6833	-0.3199
2.	Approval from societies	3.7881	3.0672	0.9697
3.	Influence of union	2.9193	2.7336	0.3492
4.	Lack of supporting document	3.8182	3.4569	0.5608
5.	Lack of income proof	3.6903	2.9987	1.2962
6.	Official formalities	2.5783	3.6069	-1.9907*
7.	Political pressure	2.6811	2.8084	-0.3126
8.	Non response from members	3.0234	3.1143	-0.1134
9.	Lack of guarantor certificate	3.4341	2.9091	0.7089
10.	Chairman's remarks	3.8217	2.9843	2.1141*
11.	Official influence	2.9106	3.2491	-0.4046

* Significant at five per cent level.

Table 5.10 indicates the important reasons for delay in sanctioning the loan by the societies. In the societies at Nagercoil, the highly viewed reasons for such a delay were chairman's remarks, lack of supporting document and approval from the societies since their mean scores were 3.8217, 3.8182 and 3.7881 respectively whereas not seriously viewed reasons were official formalities and political pressure since the respective mean scores were 2.5783 and 2.6811. In the societies at Thuckalay, the seriously viewed reasons were partially filled applications, official formalities and non response from members since the mean scores were 3.6833, 3.6069 and 3.1143 respectively whereas the lesser viewed reasons were influence of union and political pressure since the respective mean scores were 2.7336 and 2.8084. Regarding the perception on the reasons, the significant differences among the employees in two groups of societies are noticed in the case of official formalities and Chairman's remarks since the respective 't' statistics were significant at 5 per cent level.

Important Factors for Delay in Sanctioning the Loan

Factor analysis was administered to identify the important factors leading to delay in sanctioning the loan. It results in three important factors namely borrowers, official and social. The factor loading of the reasons in each factor and their reliability coefficient are presented in Table 5.11.

The extracted three factors by the factor analysis explain the eleven reasons for delay in sanctioning the loans to the extent of 66.17 per cent. The most important factor leading to the delay is 'borrowers', since its Eigen value and the per cent of variation were 3.0962 and 24.25 per cent respectively. It consists of five variables with the reliability coefficient of 0.7309. The second important factor was 'official' factor. It consists of three variables with the reliability coefficient of 0.7524. The Eigen value and the per cent of variation of this factor were 2.1676 and 21.69 per cent respectively. The last factor identified by the factor analysis was 'social' factor which consists of three variables with the reliability coefficient of 0.8717. The Eigen value and the per cent of variation explained by this factor were 1.4502 and 20.23 per cent respectively. The very important reasons in the above said three important factors were partially filled application, approval from societies and the influence of union.

Table 5.11

Factor Loading of the Reasons for Delay in Sanctioning of Loan

Factors (Eigen value)	*Reasons*	*Factor loading*	*Reliability coefficient*	*Per cent of variation*
Borrowers (3.0962)	Partially filled application	.9021	0.7309	24.25
	Lack of supporting document	.8173		
	Lack of income proof	.7304		
	Non response from members	.6557		
	Lack of guarantor certificate	.6338		
Official (2.1676)	Approval from societies	.8909	0.7524	21.69
	Official formalities	.8134		
	Chairman's remarks	.7568		
Social (1.4502)	Influence of union	.8447	0.8717	20.23
	Political pressure	.8062		
	Officers' influence	.7608		

Association Between the Profile of Employees and their Perception on Reasons for Delay

The profile of the employees may have its own role in their perception on the reasons for delay in sanctioning loan. So the present study has made an attempt to analyse the significant association between the profile of the employees and their perception on the factors leading to delay was drawn from the mean scores of the various reasons for delay in each factor. In order to find out the association, the one way analysis of variance was applied. The resulted 'F' statistics are presented in Table 5.12.

Table 5.12

Association Between the Profile of Employees and their Perception on Delay in Sanctioning Loan

Sl. No.	*Profile Variables*	*F-statistics*		
		Borrowers	*Official*	*Social*
1.	Gender	2.8681	3.9801*	2.4068
2.	Age	2.0786	2.8677*	3.1142*
3.	Level of education	2.9291*	2.3781*	2.7081*
4.	Years of experience	2.0114	1.8681	2.6408*
5.	Monthly income	2.3417	2.5496*	2.8331*
6.	Banking orientation	2.7882*	2.5093*	3.0193*

* Significant at 5 per cent level.

Regarding the perception on the borrowers, the significant difference among the staff was identified when they were classified on the basis of their level of education and banking orientation since the respective 'F' statistics were significant at five per cent level. The significant associating profile variables in the perception on the official factor leading to delay were gender, age, level of education, monthly income and banking orientation since the respective 'F' statistics were significant at 5 per cent level. In the perception of 'Social' factor, the significantly associating profile variables were age, level of education, years of experience, monthly income and banking orientation.

EMPLOYEES PERCEPTION ON THE REPAYMENT RATE IN SOCIETIES

The repayment of loan by the members in the societies determines the financial soundness of the societies. If the repayment of loans by the members is regular, it is a good symptom for the development of the society. If the default rate is high, the financial position of the society is highly questionable. The employees' perception on the repayment rate prevailing in their societies were enquired. These were confined to very good, good, moderate, poor and very poor. The distribution of employees' view on different repayment rates is shown in Table 5.13.

Table 5.13

Perception of Repayment Position

Sl. No.	Perception	*Societies at Nagercoil*		*Societies at Thuckalay*		*Total*	
		No. of Employees	*Percentage*	*No. of Employees*	*Percentage*	*No. of Employees*	*Percentage*
1.	Very good	3	6.52	2	7.69	5	6.94
2.	Good	6	13.04	3	11.54	9	12.50
3.	Moderate	5	10.87	3	11.54	8	11.11
4.	Poor	18	39.13	7	26.92	25	34.72
5.	Very poor	14	30.43	11	42.31	25	34.72
	Total	46	100.00	26	100.00	72	100.00

In total, 69.44 per cent of the total employees were of the opinion that the repayment rates in the societies were poor and very poor. Only 19.44 per cent of the employees said that the repayment rates were good and very good. In the societies at Nagercoil, the employees' perception on repayment rate was poor whereas in societies at Thuckalay, it was very poor. Very good repayment rate in the societies at Nagercoil constitutes only 6.52 per cent whereas in the societies at Thuckalay it constitutes only 7.69 per cent.

EMPLOYEES' PERCEPTION ON THE REASONS FOR DEFAULT

The reasons for default according to the perception of employees differ from the borrowers' view. In order to take appropriate measures to control the defaults in the societies, the employees' perception on the reasons for default is highly important. The reasons for default in the societies have been identified by the reviews. (Latoria, *et al.*, 1998[7] and Sharma *et al.*, 2000[8]). The identified reasons are misutilisation of loan, government policy, no proper record at office, borrowers' mindset, influence of other members, official constraints, non-cooperation of borrowers, no proper updation of accounts, influence of union, evidence of salary deduction and no follow up action. The employees were asked to rate the above said twelve reasons at five point scale with options from highly important to not at all important. The scores assigned were varying from 5 to 1 respectively.

Table 5.14

Reasons for Default

Sl. No.	*Reasons*	*Mean Score*		*'t'-Statistics*
		Societies at Nagercoil	*Societies at Thuckalay*	
1.	Mis-utilisation of Loan	3.8638	3.2714	0.8964
2.	Government policy	2.7103	3.7606	-2.1213*
3.	High indebtedness of borrowers	3.1211	2.8932	0.4093
4.	No proper records at office	2.5072	2.4311	0.1892
5.	Borrowers' mindset	3.8683	2.9192	2.0963*
6.	Influence of other members	3.2123	3.3671	-0.2161
7.	Official constraints	2.7864	2.9798	-0.1736
8.	Non-co-operation of borrowers	3.2197	3.8684	-1.2047
9.	No proper updation of accounts	2.9193	3.0863	-0.2433
10.	Influence of union	3.1104	3.2627	-0.1908
11.	Avoidance of salary deduction	3.4063	3.6761	-0.3032
12.	No follow up action	3.9717	3.8684	0.1193

* Significant at 5 per cent level.

Table 5.14 illustrates the mean scores of the various reasons among the employees in two groups of societies. The important reasons identified by the employees of the societies at Nagercoil were no follow up action, borowers' mindset and misutilisation of loan since the respective mean scores were 3.9717, 3.8683 and

3.8638. In the societies at Thuckalay, these were non-cooperation of borrowers, no follow up action and government policy since the respective mean scores were 3.8684 and 3.7606. Regarding the perception on the reasons for default, the significant differences among the employees in two groups of societies were identified in the perception on government policy and borrowers mindset since the respective 't' statistics were significant at five per cent level.

Factors Leading to Default

The important factors leading to default are found out with the help of factor analysis. The factor analysis has been administered to narrate the 12 reasons for default. The scores of each reason given by the employees have been taken into account. The factor analysis resulted in three important factors leading to default namely borrowers, official and social.

Table 5.15

Factor Loading of the Various Reasons for Default

Factors (Eigen value)	*Reasons for Default*	*Factor loading*	*Reliability coefficient*	*Per cent of variation*
Borrowers (4.1726)	Mis utilisation of loans	.8684	0.7964	25.42
	High indebtedness	.8089		
	Mindset of borrowers	.7394		
	Non-co-operation of borrowers	.7102		
	Avoid deduction from source	.6861		
Official (3.0891)	No proper records	.9331	0.8426	21.47
	No proper updation	.8284		
	No follow up action	.7963		
	Official constraints	.7132		
Social (2.0341)	Influence of union	.9098	.8508	20.08
	Influence of other members	.8162		
	Government policy	.7286		

Table 5.15 explains the factor loading of the variables in each factor and its reliability coefficient. All the three factors extracted by the factor analysis explain the reasons for default to the extent of 66.97 per cent. The most important factor was 'borrower' which consists of five reasons with the reliability coefficient of 0.7964. The Eigen value and the per cent of variation of this factor were 4.1726 and 25.42 per cent respectively. The second important factor leading to default was 'official' which consists of four variables with reliability coefficient of 0.8426. The Eigen value and the per cent of variation of this factor were 3.0891 and 21.47 per cent respectively. The last factor extracted by the factor analysis was 'Social' factor which includes three variables with the reliability coefficient of 0.8508. The Eigen value and the per cent of variation of this factor were 2.0341 and 20.08 per cent respectively.

EMPLOYEES' ATTITUDE TOWARDS THE SOCIETY

The attitude towards the society represents the employees' attitude on various functions and performance of the society. The employees' attitude is more important than any other thing for the better performance of the society. The favourable attitude on various functions of the society may lead to a better performance of the society. In the present study, an attempt was made to measure the employees' attitude towards various functions and services provided by the society. Even though the functions of the society are too many, the present study confines these function to eighteen variables. These variables were drawn from the reviews (Shankaran, 1995[9] and Ganur *et al.*, 2003[10]). The identified variables of the society are variety of deposits, atmosphere, accessibility, value added products, customer's knowledge, customers' response, officers' help, interpersonal relationship, location, variety of loans, customers' behaviour, speedy disposal, network, communication, union behaviour, policy implementation, technology used and varied rates of interest. The employees were asked to rate the above said eighteen variables at five point scale with options, highly satisfied, satisfied, moderate, dissatisfied and highly dissatisfied. The marks assigned on these options were 5, 4, 3, 2 and 1 respectively. The mean score of the attitude towards each variable was calculated to exhibit the employees' attitude towards various aspects of the society. The 't' test was used to analyse the significant differences between employees of two groups of societies regarding their attitude. The resulted mean scores on the variables of the function of society and their respective 't' statistics are shown in Table 5.16.

Table 5.16

Attitude Towards the Society

Sl. No.	*Variables in society*	*Mean Score*		*'t'-Statistics*
		Societies at Nagercoil	*Societies at Thuckalay*	
1.	Variety of deposits	2.0371	2.7682	-1.4565
2.	Atmosphere	2.3142	2.9611	-0.6086
3.	Accessibility	3.0141	2.8642	0.3089
4.	Value added products	1.8792	2.7181	-2.2191*
5.	Customers' knowledge	3.1143	2.5654	0.9098
6.	Customers' response	2.4568	2.3061	0.2718
7.	Officer's help	3.2171	2.4147	1.0869
8.	Interpersonal relationship	2.8684	2.0671	1.1174
9.	Location	2.0811	2.9648	-2.0817*
10.	Variety of loans	1.8183	2.7172	-2.1142*
11.	Customers' behaviour	3.2081	2.4561	1.9964*
12.	Speedy disposal	2.4162	3.6131	-2.7068*
13.	Network	2.0833	3.4317	-3.1142*
14.	Communication	2.2171	3.2663	-2.5086*
15.	Unions behaviour	3.4086	3.2161	0.4083
16.	Policy implementation	2.9193	3.0862	-0.2193
17.	Technology used	1.8181	2.6564	-2.1977*
18.	Variety of rates of interest	2.0214	2.3741	-0.3096

* Significant at 5 per cent level.

The moderately perceived variables among the employees in the societies at Nagercoil were union behaviour, officers' help and customer's behaviour since the respective mean scores were 3.4086, 3.2171 and 3.2081 respectively. The dissatisfied variables among them were technology used, variety of loans and value added products since the mean scores were 1.8181, 1.8183 and 1.8792 respectively. Among the employees in societies at Thuckalay, the satisfied variables were speedy disposal, network and communication since their mean scores were 3.6131, 3.4317 and 3.2663 respectively whereas moderately viewed variables were interpersonal relationship, customers' response and variety in rates of interest since the respective mean scores were 2.0671, 2.3061 and 2.3741. Regarding the attitude towards the variables of the society, the significant differences among the employees in two groups of societies have been noticed in the case of perception on value added products, location, variety of loans, customers' behaviour, speedy disposal, network, communication and technology used since the respective 't' statistics were significant at five per cent level.

Narration of the Variables into Factors

The variables of the functions of the society are narrated with the help of factor analysis. The scores of each variables in the society have been taken into account. The factor analysis discloses important factors namely human relation, customers, product and infrastructure facilities. The factor loading of the variables in the above said factors and their reliability coefficient are shown in Table 5.17.

The narrated four factors explain the attitude towards the society to the extent of 74.95 per cent. The most important factor regarding the attitude towards the society is the 'human relation' factor. It consists of five reasons with the reliability coefficient of 0.6814. The Eigen value and the per cent of variation of the factor were 4.1832 and 21.29 per cent respectively.

The next two important factors were 'customers' and 'product' with the Eigen values of 3.0691 and 2.1718 respectively. The 'customer' factor consists of four variables with the reliability coefficient of 0.7403 whereas the 'product' factor consists of four variables with the reliability coefficient of 0.7914. The last factor narrated by the factor analysis was 'infrastructural facilities' which consists of five variables with the reliability coefficient of 0.7503.

Table 5.17

Factor Loading of Attitude Towards the Society

Factors (Eigen value)	*Variables*	*Factor loading*	*Reliability coefficient*	*Per cent of variation*
Human Relation (4.1832)	Officers help	.8314	.6814	21.29
	Speedy disposal	.7906		
	Policy implementation	.7432		
	Communication	.6817		
	Interpersonal relationship	.6036		
Customers (3.0691)	Customers' knowledge	.8708	.7403	19.32
	Customers' behaviour	.8114		
	Unions' behaviour	.7308		
	Customers' response	.7116		
Product (2.1718)	Variety of deposits	.9304	.7914	17.46
	Variety of loans	.8631		
	Variety of rates of interest	.7034		
	Value added products	.6119		
Infrastructure facilities (1.2147)	Atmosphere	.9224	.7503	16.88
	Location	.8408		
	Network	.7617		
	Technology used	.7083		
	Accessibility	.6409		

OVERALL ATTITUDE TOWARDS THE SOCIETY

The overall attitude of the employees towards the society has been measured at five point scale with options, highly satisfied, satisfied, moderate, dissatisfied and highly dissatisfied. The distribution of employees according to their overall attitude is illustrated in Table 5.18.

Table 5.18
Overall Attitude Towards the Society

Sl. No.	*Overall Attitude*	*Societies at Nagercoil*		*Societies at Thuckalay*		*Total*	
		No. of Employees	*Percentage*	*No. of Employees*	*Percentage*	*No. of Employees*	*Percentage*
1.	Highly satisfied	3	6.52	2	7.69	5	6.94
2.	Satisfied	9	19.57	1	3.85	10	13.89
3.	Moderate	11	23.91	6	23.08	17	23.61
4.	Dissatisfied	10	21.74	11	42.31	21	29.17
5.	Highly dissatisfied	13	28.26	6	23.08	19	26.39
	Total	46	100.00	26	100.00	72	100.00

Source: Primary Data.

In total, only 20.83 per cent of the employees were satisfied and highly satisfied about their societies whereas 55.56 per cent of the employees were dissatisfied and highly dissatisfied. In societies at Nagercoil, 50.00 per cent of the employees were dissatisfied and highly dissatisfied whereas in the case of societies at Thuckalay, they constitute 65.39 per cent to the total. The employees have a moderate view on their society constitute 23.91 per cent in societies at Nagercoil whereas in the societies at Thuckalay, they constitute 23.08 per cent to the total.

Association Between the Profile of Employees and their Attitude Towards their Societies

The association between the profile of the employees and their attitude towards four factors namely, human relation, customers, product and infrastructural facilities has been examined with the help of one way analysis of variance. The included profile variables are gender, age, level of education, years of experience, monthly income and banking orientation. The resulted 'F' statistics are shown in Table 5.19.

Table 5.19

Association Between Profile of Employees and their Attitude Towards the Society

Sl. No.	*Profile Variables*	*F-statistics*			
		Human Relation	*Customers*	*Product*	*Infrastructural Facilities*
1.	Gender	3.1034	2.7086	2.1163	1.8189
2.	Age	2.4033	2.7681*	2.9798*	1.3081
3.	Level of education	2.4133*	2.6814*	1.8313	1.4049
4.	Years of experience	2.0982	1.7011	1.3676	2.5768*
5.	Monthly income	2.6086*	3.2714*	3.2046*	2.9141*
6.	Banking orientation	3.1141*	3.0862*	1.3068	2.1718

* Significant at 5 per cent level.

Regarding the perception on the human relation in the society, the significant associating profile variables were level of education, monthly income, and banking orientation since the respective 'F' statistics were significant at 5 per cent level. In the case of perception on customers, the significant associating profile variables were age, level of education, monthly income and banking orientation.

The significant difference among the employees was noticed when they were classified on the basis of age and monthly income regarding their perception on product. Regarding the perception on the infrastructural facilities, the significantly associating profile variables were years of experience and monthly income since the respective 'F' statistics were significant at five per cent level.

PROBLEMS ENCOUNTERED BY THE EMPLOYEES IN THE SOCIETIES

The employees working in the societies are facing so many problems related to the official procedure, customers and collection of overdues. Since the employees have current and practical knowledge on the problems in the societies, the study has made on attempt to analyse the problems encountered by the employees. Even though the problems are too many (Rao, 2002[11]) the present study confines the problems to only thirteen. These problems are drawn from the reviews and the views of the experienced employees. The identified problems are customers' knowledge, officers' responsibility, interrelationship, poor technology, customers' behaviour, no proper communication, ignorant co-workers, delay in sanctioning loan, customers' response, seeking approval from the society, no delegation, poor in decision making and customers' relationship. The above said thirteen problems were rated by the employees at five point scale with options, very serious, serious, moderate, not serious and not at all serious. The marks assigned on these options were 5, 4, 3, 2 and 1 respectively.

In order to exhibit the important problems faced by the employees, the mean scores of the problems were computed. The significant differences among the employees in two groups of societies regarding the perception of the problems have been examined with the help of 't' test. The calculated mean scores of the problems and the respective 't' statistics are shown in Table 5.20.

The highly reviewed problems among the employees of the societies at Nagercoil were interrelationship, delay in sanctioning of loan and customers' behaviour since the respective mean scores were 4.2322, 3.9114 and 3.8604, whereas the less perceived problems were seeking approval from the society and ignorant co-workers since their mean scores were 2.4514 and 2.5081 respectively.

In the societies at Thuckalay, the highly perceived problems among the employees were poor technology, and customers response since their mean scores were 4.2614 and 4.2081 respectively whereas the less perceived problems were poor in decision making and customers' knowledge since their mean scores were 2.4506 and 2.5674 respectively. Regarding the problem perception, the significant differences between the employees in two groups of societies were identified in the perception on interrelationship, poor technology, customers' behaviour, ignorant co-workers, delay in sanctioning loan and poor in decision making since the respective 't' statistics were significant at five per cent level.

Table 5.20

Problems Encountered by the Employees

Sl. No.	*Problems*	*Mean Score*		*'t'-Statistics*
		Societies at Nagercoil	*Societies at Thuckalay*	
1.	Customers knowledge	3.1142	2.5674	0.7081
2.	Officers' responsibility	2.6828	3.4541	-1.5039
3.	Interrelationship	4.2322	3.0193	2.1708*
4.	Poor technology	3.1193	4.2614	-2.0671*
5.	Customers' behaviour	3.8608	3.0676	1.9933*
6.	No proper communication	3.7617	3.5969	0.3027
7.	Ignorant co-workers	2.5081	3.4911	-2.1143*
8.	Delay in sanctioning of loan	3.9114	2.8088	2.2163*
9.	Customers' response	3.8081	4.2081	-0.4086
10.	Seeking approval from society	2.8514	3.6783	-1.3091
11.	No delegation	2.8681	3.2143	-0.7183
12.	Poor in decision making	3.6843	2.4506	2.5117*
13.	Customers' relationship	3.0917	3.4561	-0.8082

* Significant at 5 per cent level.

Important Factors in Problem Perception

The identified thirteen problems in society are narrated into a few important factors with the help of factor analysis for further studies. The scores of the problem perception on the thirteen problems in the society have been taken into consideration for factor analysis. The factor analysis results in three important factors (problems) namely official, human relation and customers. The variables included in each factor, factor loading of the variables, their reliability coefficient, Eigen value of the factors and the per cent of variation of the factors are shown in Table 5.21.

Table 5.21

Factor Loading of the Problems Encountered by the Employees

Factors (Eigen value)	*Problems*	*Factor loading*	*Reliability coefficient*	*Per cent of variation*
Official (3.1713)	Officers' responsibility	0.9364	0.6834	24.71
	Delay in sanctioning loans	0.8601		
	No delegation	0.7314		
	No proper communication	0.6272		
	Seeking approval from society	0.5969		
Human Relations (2.4541)	Inter personal relationship	0.8414	0.7086	20.30
	Ignorant co-workers	0.7009		
	Poor technology	0.6324		
	Poor in decision making	0.5992		
Customers (1.3069)	Customers' knowledge	0.9232	0.7968	18.49
	Customers' behaviour	0.8604		
	Customers' response	0.7317		
	Customers' relationship	0.6909		

The narrated three factors explain the included problems in the societies to the extent of 63.50 per cent. The most important problem was 'official factor' which includes five problems with the reliability coefficient of 0.6834. The Eigen value and the per cent of variation of the factor were 3.1713 and 24.71 per cent respectively. The second important factor was 'human relation' factor which consists of four problems with the reliability coefficient of 0.7086. The Eigen value and the per cent of variation of the factor are 2.4541 and 20.30 per cent. The last important problem was 'customer problem'. It consists of four problems with the reliability coefficient of 0.7968. The Eigen value and the per cent of variation of the factor were 1.3069 and 18.49 per cent respectively. The important problems in the above said three factors were officers' responsibility, inter personal relationship and customers' knowledge since the respective problems had higher factor loading in the respective factor.

Association Between the Profile of the Employees and their Perception on Problems

The profile of the employees may have its own impact on the problem perception among them. In order to understand the nature of problems faced by the employees, the scores of the problem perception on each factor have been computed. The scores on each problem factor were drawn from the mean scores of the problems in each factor (important problem). The included profile variables were gender, age, level of education, years of experience, monthly income and banking orientation among the staff. In order to analyse the significant differences among the employees regarding their problem perception, the one way analysis of variance was used. The resulted 'F' statistics are shown in Table 5.22.

Table 5.22

Association Between the Profile of Employees and their Problem Perception

Sl. No.	*Profile Variables*	*F-statistics*		
		Official	*Human Relations*	*Customers*
1.	Gender	2.1781	2.9093	3.1173
2.	Age	2.4017	2.6671*	2.8082*
3.	Level of education	2.8023*	1.7183	2.4143*
4.	Years of experience	1.4146	2.2691	2.0817
5.	Monthly income	2.7183*	2.8086*	2.9194*
6.	Banking orientation	1.3064	2.9193*	2.0367

* Significant at 5 per cent level.

Regarding the perception of official problems, the significantly associating profile variables were level of education and monthly income since the respective 'F' statistics were significant at 5 per cent level. In the case of perception on human relation problem, the significant differences among the employees were estimated when they were classified on the basis of age, monthly income and banking orientation. Regarding the perception on the customer problem, the significantly associating profile variables were age, level of education and monthly income since the respective 'F' statistics were significant at five per cent level.

Impact of Problem Perception on Overall Attitude Towards the Society

The problem perception among the employees has its own role in the formation of attitude towards the society. In general, the employees highly perceived the problems result in a poor attitude towards the society. Similarly, the less perception on problems among the employees results in a higher attitude towards the society. The present analysis attempts to examine the impact of perceptions of important problems on the overall attitude towards the society among the employees. The score on the overall attitude towards the society was taken as the score of dependent variable, whereas the scores on problem perceptions on official, human relation and customers were taken as the scores of independent variables. The multiple regression analysis has been used to analyse the impact. The fitted regression model is

$$y = a+b_1x_1+b_2x_2+b_3x_3+e$$

whereas y = Score on overall attitude towards the society

x_1 = Score on the perception of official problem

x_2 = Score on the perception of human relation problem

x_3 = Score on the perception of customer problem

b_1, b_2, b_3 = Regression coefficients of independent variables

a = Constant and

e = Error terms.

The impact analysis is carried among the employees of societies at Nagercoil and Thuckalay and also for pooled data separately. The results are shown in Table 5.23.

Table 5.23

Impact of Problem Perception on Overall Attitude Towards Society

Sl. No.	*Independent Variables*	*Regression Coefficients*		
		Societies at Nagercoil	*Societies at Thuckalay*	*Pooled*
1.	Official	-0.1834*	-0.2146*	-0.1904*
2.	Human Relation	0.0342	-0.3083*	-0.2023*
3.	Customers	-0.2968*	-0.1131	-0.1704*
	Constant	0.1711	-0.2714	-0.1146
	R^2	0.6804	0.6293	0.7277
	F-Statistics	9.3082*	8.0814*	10.3908*

* Significant at 5 per cent level.

In societies at Nagercoil, the significant influencing problem perceptions were official and customer problems. A unit increase in the perception on the above two problems results in a decrease in overall attitude towards the society by 0.1834 and 0.2968 units respectively. In societies at Thuckalay, the significant influencing problem perceptions were official and human relation problems since their regression coefficients were significant at five per cent level. It reveals that a unit increase in the perception on the above two problems results in a decrease in overall attitude towards the society by 0.2146 and 0.3083 units respectively.

The analysis of pooled data revealed that a unit increase in the perception on official, human relation and customers related problems results in a decrease in overall attitude towards the society by 0.1904, 0.2023 and 0.1704 units respectively. The change in problem perception explains the change in overall attitude towards the society to the extent of 72.77 per cent. The significant 'F' statistics reveals the viability of fitted regression model.

MEASURES TO IMPROVE THE SOCIETY

The employees of the societies have a lot of experience and knowledge regarding the societies. So they are the real judges to decide on the measures to be taken to improve the society. Even though the measures to be taken for the improvement of the society are too many, the present study includes only nineteen measures. All these measures are identified with the help of reviews (Rene, 1991[12] and Singh 2002[13]).

The identified measures are delegation, loan amount, training to employees, quick processing, knowledgeable employees, customers' relationship, proper communication, variety of loans, counselling at pre loan period, better salary flexibility, variety of rates of interest, knowledgeable officer, welfare facilities to employees, repayment period, customers' education, inter personal relationship, modern technology and value added service. The employees were asked to rate the above said measures at five point scale with options from highly important to not at all important. The scores assigned on the scales vary from 5 to 1. The mean scores of the measures have been computed to reveal the importance of the measures.

Table 5.24 explains the importance of included measures to improve the society. In the societies at Nagercoil, the highly reviewed measures to improve the societies were customers' relationship, modern technology and quick processing since the respective mean scores were 3.8183, 3.8114 and 3.7174. Whereas in the societies at Thuckalay, these measures were better salary, inter personal relationship and welfare facilities to the employees since their mean scores were 3.8684, 3.6817 and 3.4768 respectively. Regarding the view on the measures to promote the societies, there is no significant difference among the employees in two groups of societies since the respective 't' statistics are not significant at 5 per cent level. It infers that the employee in two groups of societies revealed the same views on the measures to be taken to improve the societies.

Table 5.24

Measures to Improve the Societies

Sl. No.	*Measures*	*Mean Score*		*'t'-Statistics*
		Societies at Nagercoil	*Societies at Thuckalay*	
1.	Delegation	2.9192	[illegible]863	-0.2317
2.	Loan amount	3.4341	2.9146	0.6081
3.	Training to employees	3.6086	3.1139	0.8182
4.	Quick processing	3.7174	3.3563	0.5096
5.	Knowledgeable employees	3.0826	2.9194	0.1708
6.	Customer's relationship	3.8183	3.0311	1.8314
7.	Proper communication	2.9405	3.2627	-0.5058
8.	Variety of loans	3.4093	2.7679	0.6196
9.	Counselling at pre loan period	2.8681	3.0897	-0.2387
10.	Better salary	3.6162	3.8684	-0.3919
11.	Flexibility	2.9193	3.4014	-0.6187
12.	Variety of rates of interest	3.4022	3.0896	0.5239
13.	Knowledgeable officer	3.1142	2.8963	0.4644
14.	Welfare facilities to employees	2.9691	3.4768	-0.6167
15.	Repayment period	2.4514	3.0671	-0.5829
16.	Customers' education	2.8286	3.1144	-0.4914
17.	Interpersonal relationship	3.1917	3.6817	-0.6317
18.	Modern technology	3.8114	3.0642	1.3231
19.	Value added service	2.9083	3.1163	-0.3962

* Significant at 5 per cent level.

Narration of the Measures to Improve the Society

The included nineteen measures to improve the society were narrated with the help of factor analysis. The score on each measure by the employees has been included for the factor analysis. The factor analysis results in four important factors to be taken for the improvement of societies. These are product, employee, management and customers factors. The measures included in each factor, their factor loading and the reliability coefficient of the factors are exhibited in Table 5.25.

Table 5.25

Factor Loading of Measures to Improve the Society

Factors (Eigen value)	*Suggestions*	*Factor loading*	*Reliability coefficient*	*Per cent of variation*
Product (3.6121)	Variety of loans	0.8681	0.7082	23.86
	Loan amount	0.8239		
	Variety of rates of interest	0.7396		
	Repayment period	0.7127		
	Flexibility	0.6803		
	Value added services	0.6441		
Employee (2.9307)	Training to employee	0.9317	0.7386	21.32
	Knowledgeable employee	0.8608		
	Better remuneration	0.7291		
	Welfare facilities to employee	0.6417		
	Inter personal relationships	0.6224		
Management (2.5663)	Delegation	0.8719	0.7271	20.19
	Quick processing	0.8108		
	Proper communication	0.7334		
	Knowledgeable officer	0.7161		
	Modern technology	0.6883		
Customers (1.8184)	Customers' education	0.8917	0.8231	18.86
	Counselling at pre-loan period	0.8162		
	Customers' relation	0.7508		

The narrated four important factors explain the measures to improve the societies to the extent of 84.23 per cent. The most important factor was 'product' factor which consists of six measures with the reliability coefficient of 0.7082. The Eigen value and the per cent of variation of the factor were 3.6121 and

23.86 per cent respectively. The second important factor was the 'employee' factor which consists of five measures with the reliability coefficient of 0.7386. The third important factor namely 'management' factor consists of five measures with the reliability coefficient of 0.7271. The Eigen value and the per cent of variation of this factor are 2.5663 and 20.19 per cent respectively. The last factor namely 'customer' factor consists of three measures with the reliability coefficient of 0.8231. The most important measures in the above said four factors are variety of loans, training to employees, delegation and customers' education since their respective factor loading were higher in the respective factor.

Association Between the Profile of Employees and their View on Improvement

The employees' views on the improvement was analysed at four different dimensions namely improvement in product, employees, management and customers. The scores of the views on the above said four important factors were drawn from the mean scores of the various measures in each factor. Regarding the employees views for improvement of societies, to reveal the significant differences among them under different profile classification, the one way analysis of variance was administered. The resulted 'F' statistics are presented in Table 5.26.

Table 5.26

Association Between the Profile of the Employees and their Suggestions

Sl. No.	*Profile Variables*	*F-statistics*			
		Product	*Employees*	*Management*	*Customers*
1.	Gender	1.8917	2.0676	2.3714	2.8981
2.	Age	2.5142	2.9237*	1.3881	2.0246
3.	Level of education	2.3917*	1.3086	2.0334	2.5718*
4.	Years of experience	2.6708*	2.9173*	2.1408	2.8034*
5.	Monthly income	1.9142	2.0671	1.9969	2.6738*
6.	Banking orientation	2.8108*	1.3407	2.2711	2.8681*

* Significant at 5 per cent level.

The significantly associating profile variables regarding the employees' views on product were level of education, years of experience and banking orientation since the respective 'F' statistics were significant at 5 per cent level. Regarding the views on employees, the significantly associating profile variables were age and years of experience. Regarding the views on customers, the significant differences among the employees were identified when they were classified on the basis of level of education, years of experience, monthly income and banking orientation.

SUMMARY

Analysis of employees' profile and attitude revealed that maximum number of employees were male. The dominant age group was 41–50 years, the common level of education was graduation and the main ranges of experience was 11–15 years. Their overall attitude towards the society was dissatisfied. Their suggestions for the improvement were product, employees, management and customers.

REFERENCES

1. Elumalai, K., "Recent Trends in Co-operative Legislations in India', in Positioning Co-operatives in 21st Century", *Proceedings of National Symposium, Vaikunth Mehta National Institute of Co-operative Management*, Pune, 1999, pp. 89-101.

2. Shah and Deepak, "Co-operative Dairying in Maharashtra: Lessons to be Learned", *Economic and Political Weekly*, 32(39), September 1997, pp. 125-135.

3. Jugale and V. Band Pail, D.T., "Co-operative Credit and Agricultural Change: A Case Study", In: *India's Small Co-operatives*, Gurcharan Kainth (ed), Regency Publications, New Delhi, 1998.

4. Lal, R.C., and Lavania, "Impact of Cooperative Credit on Agriculture Production and Income", *Indian Cooperative Review*, 23(3), 1986, pp. 264-276.

5. Singh, S.K., Singh, R.I., and Singh, G.N., "Impact of rural Cooperative Credit on Agricultural Development in Eastern UP", *Indian Cooperative Review*, 27(1), 1989, pp. 210-216.

6. Palanisamy, A., and Arunachalam, "Utilisation and Repayment of Cooperative Crop Loan", *Indian Cooperative Review*, 29(2), 1991, pp. 180-186.

7. Latoria, S.K., Janlkar, A.M., and Sush, V.N., "Repayment Performance of Agricultural Credit Users in Gwaliar District (M.P)", *Land Bank Journal*, 25(1), 1998, pp. 55-60.

8. Sharma, S.K., Daipura, O.P., Janlkar, A.M., and Latoria, S.K., "An Analysis of Overdues and Repayment Behaviour of Agricultural Credit", *Land Bank Journal*, December 2000, pp. 45-49.

9. Shankaran, P.N., "Performance of Primary Cooperative Agricultural Development Banks in Kerala: A Model for Quantitative Analysis", *Indian Cooperative Review*, 33(1), 1995, pp. 15-20.

10. Ganur, B.N., Sale, D.L., and Kale, N.K., "Performance of Cooperative Banks in Supply of Loans to the Farmers in Maharashtra", *The Maharashtra Cooperative Quarterly*, 89(4), 2003, pp. 25-34.

11. Akula Rajagopala Rao, "Employees' Attitude Towards Cooperatives and Facilities in Urban Cooperative Banks: A Study", *Indian Cooperative Review*, 40(2), October 2002, pp. 108-118.

12. Rene, T., "True Productivity – The Key to Profitability", *Executive digest*, December 1991, pp. 9-14.

13. Katar Singh, "Cooperatives Emerging Chalenges and Coping Strategies", *Kurukshetra*, November 2002, pp. 16-21.

6

SUMMARY OF FINDINGS, CONCLUSIONS AND SUGGESTIONS

INTRODUCTION

The objectives of the present study were accomplished in three stages. First of all, the performance of Employees Cooperative Thrift and Credit Societies at Nagercoil and Thuckalay were analysed. It was followed by a study on the members' attitudes towards the societies and the problems encountered by them. In the third stage, the employees' attitude towards the societies, problems encountered by them and the measures to improve the functioning of the societies were analysed. Results of the analysis were presented and discussed in the earlier chapters. The work done and its findings are summarised in this chapter to draw specific inferences and their policy implications.

The specific objectives of this study were:

(i) To appraise the working of the Employees' Cooperative Thrift and Credit Societies in Kanyakumari District;

(ii) To study the profile of the members of ECTCS, their attitude towards the society, association between their

profile and attitude, their problems and the suggestions provided by them for the improvement of the societies;

(iii) To exhibit the profile of the employees of ECTCS, their attitude towards the society, their problems, the relationship between their profile and their attitude and the suggestions provided by them for the improvement of the societies; and

(iv) To offer suggestions based on the findings of the study.

The concepts and methodology were formulated according to the objectives of the study with the help of comprehensive review of previous studies. The secondary data about the performance of the ECTCS, were collected from reports and records of the societies.

For the primary data, all the ECTCS which keep the financial records for the past 10 years were purposively selected for the study. By that, out of the total societies of 26 and 15 at Nagercoil and Thuckalay, only 23 and 13 societies were selected. From the total members of the societies in the above said two areas, the total sample of 2 per cent of total members was arbitrarily assigned. The determined 564 sample members were proportionally distributed in the above said 23 and 13 societies at Nagercoil and Thuckalay. The random sampling method was applied to select the samples from each society. In order to study, the employees' perception on the societies, from each society, two employees were selected at random. So the sample size of employees was 72. The selected respondents (members and employees) were contacted in person and required data were collected with the help of a pre-tested comprehensive schedule.

A profile of the study area presented a descriptive account which includes the socio-economic profile of the district. Collected data were analysed with the help of appropriate tools to examine the performance of the societies, the association between the profile of respondents and their attitude towards the societies.

FINDINGS

The findings of the present study were classified under three headings namely findings regarding the financial aspects of the ECTCS, findings regarding the members of ECTCS and findings related to the employees of ECTCS.

Findings Regarding the Financial Aspects of ECTCS

The number of members of the societies was increasing from 1994-95 to 1999-2000. From 2000-01 onwards the number of members of the societies was declining because of the stagnation of the new appointment in Governmental organisation. The compound growth rates of share capital of the societies at Nagercoil and Thuckalay during the study period were 13.55 and 15.07 per cent respectively.

The mean of deposits of the societies at Nagercoil increased around three times whereas in case of the societies at Thuckalay, it increased around two times. The mean of loan disbursed by the societies at Nagercoil increased around 2.5 times whereas in case of the societies at Thuckalay, it increased by around 4.5 times during the period of the study. The compound growth rates of deposits and loans of the societies at Nagercoil were 9.93 and 12.43 per cent respectively whereas in the societies at Thuckalay, these two compound growth rates were 21.84 and 15.14 per cent respectively.

The mean of spread in the societies at Nagercoil, increased from Rs. 3.18 lakh in 1994-95 to Rs. 7.06 lakh in 2003-04 whereas in the case of societies at Thuckalay, the mean of spread increased from Rs. 2.24 lakh to Rs. 8.36 lakh. The compound growth rates of share investments and other investments made by the societies at Nagercoil were 10.81 and 19.03 per cent respectively whereas in the societies at Thuckalay, the compound growth rates were 18.47 and 44.35 per cent respectively.

The mean of bank loans borrowed by the society from Kanyakumari District Central Cooperative Bank (KDCCB) increased from Rs. 3.39 lakh in 1994-95 to 27.74 lakh in 2003-04 whereas in the societies at Thuckalay, it increased from Rs. 16.46 lakh to 94.43 lakh respectively. The compound growth rate of bank loan borrowed by the societies at Nagercoil during the period of the study was 23.72 per cent, whereas at Thuckalay, this was 17.13 per cent. The compound growth rates of non-statutory reserve made by the societies at Nagercoil and Thuckalay were 17.72 and 43.45 per cent respectively.

The compound growth rate of doubtful loan was greater than the compound growth rate of good loan in the societies at Nagercoil. In the case of societies at Thuckalay the compound growth rate of doubtful loan was greater than the compound growth rate of good loan. The compound growth rates of other incomes and establishment and contingent expenses in the societies at Nagercoil were 14.75 and 12.43 per cent respectively whereas in societies at Thuckalay, the compound growth rates were 21.21 and 15.38 per cent respectively.

The mean of interest due increased from Rs. 2.19 lakh in 1994-95 to Rs. 6.59 lakh in 2003-04 at Nagercoil whereas at Thuckalay, it increased from Rs.1.16 lakh to Rs. 3.47 lakh. The compound growth rates of interest due in the societies at Nagercoil and Thuckalay were 13.60 and 11.69 per cent respectively. Regarding the interest overdue, the compound growth rates in the societies at Nagercoil and Thuckalay were 22.24 and 32.60 per cent respectively.

The compound growth rates of net profit in the societies at Nagercoil and Thuckalay were 15.53 and 17.79 per cent respectively whereas in the case of undistributed profit, the compound growth rates were 15.60 and 41.89 per cent respectively. The compound growth rates of sundry debtors in the societies at Nagercoil and Thuckalay were 29.95 and 24.30 per cent respectively whereas regarding the sundry creditors, they were 29.95 and 26.14 per cent respectively.

The compound growth rates of cash in hand in the societies at Nagercoil and Thuckalay were 14.02 and 7.59 per cent respectively. The compound growth rates of cash at bank, in the societies at these two places were –5.97 and 5.17 per cent respectively. The compound growth rates of investment on furniture in the societies at Nagercoil and Thuckalay were 5.95 and 14.08 per cent respectively.

All the above said variables were only increasing in the case of the societies at Nagercoil and Thuckalay except the variable number of members.

Regarding the economic viability of the societies at Nagercoil, majority of the societies have a mean ratio of overdue to its demand of less than 40 per cent. The mean of overdues to demand in the societies at Nagercoil decreased from 38.38 per cent in 1994-95 to 22.03 per cent in 2003-04. In the case of Thuckalay societies, the mean of overdues to demand was declined from 24.51 per cent to 24.29 per cent during the same period. Majority of the societies have a mean of overdue ratio of less than 40 per cent.

The operational efficiency of the societies was examined with help of own funds to borrowed funds, borrowed funds to working capital, credit to deposit and outstanding loans to working capital. The operational efficiency was identified as higher in the societies at Thuckalay since the first three ratios were higher in those societies and the outstanding loans to working capital was also less in that societies.

The financial efficiency of the societies was evaluated by the total expenses to total income, net profit to working capital, interest paid to interest received and non-interest expenses to non-interest income. Regarding the total expenses to total income, interest paid to interest received and non-interest expenses to non-interest income, the means of the ratios were identified as higher and the net profit to working capital was less in the case of the societies at Thuckalay.

The liquidity efficiency of the societies was examined by the cash in hand, bank to borrowed funds, investments to deposits and spread to total assets. Regarding the first ratio, the societies at Nagercoil were better than the societies at Thuckalay. But in the case of investments to deposits and spread to total assets, the societies at Thuckalay were better than the societies at Nagercoil.

The significant influencing variables on the net profit of the societies at Nagercoil were reserve fund, working capital, overdues and spread. The increase in spread will result in an increase in net profit of the societies. But the increase in reserve fund, working capital and overdue will result in a decrease in net profit of the societies. In the societies at Thuckalay, the significant influencing variables on the net profit of the societies were reserve fund, advances, working capital, overdues and spread. The increase in spread and advances result in an increase in net profit of the societies whereas the increase in reserve fund, working capital and overdues result in a decrease in net profit of the societies.

In general the analysis of the financial aspects of ECTCS revealed that the financial position of the societies was good.

Findings Regarding the Members of ECTCS

The analysis of the members' profile, attitude, their problems and association between their profile and attitude resulted in the following findings.

The maximum members of the societies were males. The dominant age group among the members were 41 to 45 years and 46 to 50 years. The common levels of education among the members were Graduation and post graduation. The dominant occupations among the members were clerical assistants and teachers. One-third of the selected members in the present study have subsidiary occupation apart from their main occupation. The important subsidiary occupations among the members were agriculture and finance.

Regarding marital status most of the members of the societies were 'married'. Most of the members' personal income per month ranges from Rs.10,001 to 15,000 and Rs. 5,000 to 10,000.

The important levels of media exposure among the members were very high and high whereas levels of sociability among them were moderate and high. The important levels innovativeness were very low and low. In the credit orientation, the important levels among the members were moderate and low and in the scientific orientation, these two levels were very low and low. The common personality indices of the members were 41 to 60 per cent and 20 to 40 per cent.

The dominant levels of family income per month among the members were Rs. 10,001 to 14,000; Rs. 14,001 to 18,000 and Rs. 6,000 to 10,000. Maximum number of members of the societies

The important reasons for defaults among the members of the societies at Nagercoil were mismanagement of debts and unexpected financial problem whereas in societies at Thuckalay, the two main reasons were unexpected financial problem and higher monthly instalment. Regarding the perception on the various reasons for defaults, the significant differences among the members in two groups of societies were identified regarding the perception on family problems, leniency in recovery, higher monthly instalment, unexpected sickness, mismanagement of debts and expectation to write off.

The important factors leading to default among the members identified by the factor analysis were environmental factor, financial factor and personal factor. The significantly influencing factors among the members of the societies at Nagercoil and Thuckalay were financial and personal factors.

The important service quality factors narrated by the factor analysis were time, interaction, infrastructural facilities and product factors. The higher mean differences between the expectation and perception on product and time have been identified among the members of the societies at Nagercoil and Thuckalay.

Regarding the overall attitude towards the societies, the important attitudes were dissatisfied and moderate. Regarding the overall attitude, the significantly associating profile variables were age, level of education, personal income, family income and personality index. The significant influencing perceptions of service quality factors on the overall attitude towards the society were time and interaction in societies at Nagercoil whereas in societies at Thuckalay, these were time, interaction and product. The increase in the perception on the service quality factors results in an increase in overall attitude towards the society.

The main preferences among the members on the continuation of membership in the societies were disliking and high disliking. The important reasons for their disliking to be the members in case of societies at Nagercoil were low loan amount, high rate of interest and unreliable service whereas in societies at Thuckalay, these were unreliable service, high rate of interest and poor administration. Regarding the perception on the reasons for disliking, the significant differences among the members in two groups of societies have been noticed in the perceptions on strained relationship with staff, poor administration, poor modernisation and less service quality.

The important factors leading to disliking to be the members at the society were service quality, official formalities, product and finance factors. The most important factor identified was service quality.

The important problems encountered by the members in the societies at Nagercoil were poor service quality, higher rate of interest and procedural formalities whereas in the societies at Thuckalay, these were unreality on the service, procedural formalities and poor knowledge among the staff. Regarding the problem perception, the significant differences among the members in two groups of societies have been identified in the perception on higher rate of interest, limited working hours, lack of communication and unreliability on the service.

Important problems of the members identified by the factor analysis were office formalities, service quality, staff and product factors and the most important factor identified by the factor analysis was the 'office formalities'.

Regarding the perception on office formalities, the significant associating profile variables were level of education, personal income, family income and personality index.

Analysis of the impact of problem perception on overall attitude towards the society revealed that the increase in the problem perception results in a decrease in overall attitude towards the society.

For the improvement of the societies, the important measures identified by members of the societies at Nagercoil were wider range of products, improvement in reliability and regularity in payment of dividend whereas in the societies at Thuckalay, these were increase in loan amount, appointment of knowledgeable staff and various rates of interest. Regarding the opinion on the measures for the improvement in societies, the significant differences among the members in two groups of societies were identified in the perception on wider range of products, various rates of interest and follow up actions.

The important factors leading to the improvement of the societies identified by the factor analysis were office work, staff and product.

Findings Regarding the Employees of ECTCS

The analysis of the employees' profile, attitude, association between their profile and attitude, problems encountered by them and their suggestions for the improvement of the societies resulted in the following findings.

The maximum number of employees working in the societies were males. The dominant age groups among the employees were 41 to 50 years and above 50 years. The most common level of education among them was Graduation. The main ranges of years of experience of the employees of the societies at Nagercoil and Thuckalay were 11 to 15 years and 5 to 10 years.

The levels of monthly income of the employees were Rs. 2,000 to 4,000 and Rs. 4,001 to 6,000. The common level of monthly income among the employees of the societies at Nagercoil was above Rs. 8,000 whereas in the case of societies at Thuckalay, it was only Rs. 2,000 to 4,000. Most of the employees were moderate to poor in the banking orientation. The common level of banking orientation among the employees of the societies at Nagercoil was moderate whereas in case of societies at Thuckalay, it was poor.

The important variables considered for sanction of loan in the societies at Nagercoil were income certificate, guarantor certificate and credit worthiness whereas in the societies at Thuckalay, these were loan amount, repayment period and mortgages. Regarding the perception on the variables considered for sanction of loan, the significant differences among the employees in two groups of societies were identified in the perceptions on income certificate, guarantor certificate and loan amount.

The important factors considered to sanction the loan were narrated by the factor analysis namely security, loan, personal and social factors. The most important factor was security factor which consists of four variables with the reliability coefficient of 0.8134 and the variation explained by this factor was 22.46 per cent.

The important reasons for the delay in sanctioning of loan in case of societies at Nagercoil were Chairman's remarks, lack of supporting document and approval from the societies whereas in the case of societies at Thuckalay, these were partially filled applications, official formalities and non response form members. Regarding the opinion on the reasons for delay, the significant differences among the employees in two groups of societies were identified in the case of official formalities and Chairman's remarks.

The important factors (reasons) for delay in sanctioning loan were narrated by the factor analysis as borrowers, official and social reasons. The most important factor for the delay was borrowers. It consists of five variables namely partially filled application, lack of supporting documents, lack of income proof, non-response from members and lack of guarantor certificate. Regarding the perception on the borrowers factor, the significant associating profile variables were level of education and banking orientation whereas in the perception on official factor, these were gender, age, level of education, monthly income and banking orientation. Regarding the perception on social factor, the significant associating profile variables were age, level of education, years of experience, monthly income and banking orientation.

The important reasons for default identified by the employees of the societies at Nagercoil were no-follow up action, borrowers' mindset and misutilisation of loan whereas in the societies at Thuckalay, these were non-cooperation of borrowers, no follow up action and government policy. Regarding the opinion on the reasons for default, the significant differences among the staff in two groups of societies were identified in the perceptions on government policy and borrowers' mindset.

The factor analysis narrated the reasons for default into three important factors namely borrowers, official and social factors. The most important factor for default was borrowers. The per cent of variation of this factor was 25.42.

When the attitude of the employees towards the society was analysed, the mean scores regarding the attitude revealed that, the relatively better perceived variables among the employees of the societies at Nagercoil were union behaviour, officer's help and customer's behaviour whereas among the employees of the societies at Thuckalay, these were speedy disposal, network and communication.

Factor analysis of the attitude towards the society, narrated four factors namely, human relation, customers, product and infrastructure facilities. Regarding the perception on human relation factor, the significantly associating profile variables were level of education, monthly income and banking orientation whereas in the perception on customers, these profile variables were age, level of education, monthly income and banking orientation. In the perception on product factor, these significant profile variables are age and monthly income whereas in the perception of infrastructural facilities, these profile variables were years of experience and monthly income.

The important problems identified by the employees of the societies at Nagercoil were inter relationship, delay in sanctioning of loan and customers' behaviour whereas in the case of societies at Thuckalay, these were poor technology, customers' response and delay in sanctioning of loan. Regarding the problem perception, the significant difference among the employees of two groups of societies was noticed in the case of poor technology, customers' behaviour, ignorant co-workers, delay in sanctioning of loan and poor decision-making.

The factor analysis narrated the problems encountered by the staff in the societies into three important factors namely official, human relation and customers oriented problems. The most important problem was official factor with 24.71 per cent of variation and the second factor was human relation with 20.30 per cent of variation. Regarding the perception on the official problem, the significant associating profile variables were level of education and monthly income whereas in the perception on the human relation oriented problems, these profile variables were age, monthly income and banking orientation. Regarding the perception on the customer oriented problems, the significant associating profile variables were age, level of education and monthly income.

The significant influencing problem perceptions on the overall attitude towards the societies among the employees in societies at Nagercoil were perceptions on official and customers oriented problems whereas in societies at Thuckalay, these were perception on official and human relation oriented problems. In all cases, the increase in the perception on the above said problems results in a decrease in overall attitude towards the society.

The important measures identified by the employees to improve the functioning of the societies at Nagercoil were customers' relationship, modern technology and quick processing whereas in the case of societies at Thuckalay, these were better salary, inter personal relationship and welfare facilities to the employees. Regarding the opinion on the measures for the improvement of the societies, there was no significant difference among the employees of societies at Nagercoil and Thuckalay.

The improvement measures identified by the employees were narrated by the factor analysis into four important factors namely product, staff, management and customers. The first factor for the improvement of the society was product factor with 23.86 per cent of variation. The second factor was staff factor with 21.32 per cent of variation. Regarding the opinion on the product factor, the significant associating profile variables were level of education, years of experience and banking orientation whereas in the perception on staff factor, these profile variables were age and years of experience. Regarding the perception on customers factors, the significantly associating profile variables were level of education, years of experience, monthly income and banking orientation.

POLICY IMPLICATIONS

Based on the findings of the study, the following suggestions are to be carried out to strengthen the ECTCS.

One of the main weakness of ECTCS is the lack of professionalism due to which in many cases the Board can not make efficient use of funds. The National and State level apex bodies should take initiatives to introduce professionalism in their member societies by providing training so that the societies can use their funds effectively in these days of competition.

An advisory body may be formed with professional persons either from the Board of Directors or from outside. For example, an accountant, a lawyer or a financial expert may be included in this body.

To face competition the cooperative societies should make the best use of information technology and computerise their functioning at the earliest.

Election should be conducted regularly. The Boards should be given freedom with regard to decision-making and steps should be taken to overcome political interference.

Every cooperative society may be given freedom to take up any type of business activity to make it more competitive. For instance a credit society should be allowed to launch a wholesale or retail trade in commodities or in manufacturing business.

To make the cooperative societies more efficient, management audit should be conducted every year. Cooperative societies should be encouraged to avail loans from outside financial institutions.

Regulations should be modified as to allow a primary level cooperative society to extend loan to other primary level cooperative societies and even avail loan from them.

Quick sanctioning of loan is very essential for the societies to face the competition from private banks and commercial banks. Loan sanctioning formalities may be reduced to facilitate the societies to sanction loan within a few days.

The societies may be allowed to extend loan to the sons/ daughters of the members for the purpose of starting and/or running a business unit. The concerned member may become the guarantor for the loan.

Central Government may be asked to conduct survey on different types of cooperatives and to ascertain their role in the growth of economy and also to improve their own functioning.

There is a necessity for keeping the membership of at least 200 to begin with and a minimum amount of loan transaction within one or two years to be considered viable with ability to meet the cost of a paid secretary, rent and other establishment and contingent charges. Employees of small establishment for whom separate credit societies are not feasible, may be advised to join the nearest ECTCS

The quantum of special loan for the purchase of consumer durables, purchase of sites, etc. is normally considerable and the member has to remit a sizeable amount as share capital. The members who find it difficult to remit the required share capital in cash, approach private lenders for raising the needed funds at exorbitant rate of interest. With a view to mitigate this hardship that the members are undergoing now in the remittance of the required share capital, the societies may make necessary changes in their bye-laws.

CONCLUSION

The present study concludes that the performance of the Employees Cooperative Thrift and Credit Societies are functioning better than other cooperative societies since the percentage of overdues are less. But the membership in ECTCS is sharply declining because of the stagnation of the appointment of new employees in governmental organisation. Even though the ECTCS are earning profit, they are gradually losing the confidence among their members and the staff. The general attitude towards the ECTCS among the members and the staff are not favourable because of several functioning aspects of the societies. If the problems are properly rectified by the concerned authorities, the prospects of these societies will be exemplary.

BIBLIOGRAPHY

BOOKS

Elumalai, K., "Recent Trends in Co-operative Legislations in India", In: *Positioning Co-operatives in 21st Century", Proceedings of National Symposium,* Vaikunth Mehta National Institute of Co-operative Management, Pune, 1999.

Jaya S. Anand, *Cooperative Agriculture and Rural Development Banks,* Atlantic Publishers and Distributors, New Delhi, 1999.

Joshi, G.V., *Overdues in Cooperative Credit Sector,* Mohit Publications, New Delhi, 2002.

Jugale and V. Band Pail, D.T., "Co-operative Credit and Agricultural Change: A Case Study", In: *India's Small Co-operatives,* Gurcharan Kainth (ed), Regency Publications, New Delhi, 1998.

Kamat, G.S., *New Dimensions of Cooperative Management,* Himalaya Publishing House, Bombay, 1987.

Kothari, C.R., *Research Methodology – Methods and Techniques,* Wiley Eastern Ltd., New Delhi, 1990.

Krishnamurthy, G., *Management of Cooperative Credit*, Sarangi Publishing House, Warangal, A.P., 1984.

Pondey, I.M., *Management Accounting*, Vikas Publishing House (P) Ltd., New Delhi, 1983.

Sharma, B.A.V., *et al.*, *Research Methods in Social Sciences*, Sterling Publishers Pvt. Ltd., New Delhi, 1983.

Srinivas Rao, *Cooperative Banking in New Millennium*, Anmol Publication Pvt. Ltd., New Delhi, 2004.

Wilkinson, T.S., and Bhandarkar, P.L., *Methodology and Techniques of Social Research*, Himalaya Publishing House, Bombay, 1979.

JOURNALS

Rao, Akula Rajagopala, "Employees' Attitude Towards Co-operatives and Facilities in Urban Co-operative Banks: A Case Study", *Indian Co-operative Review*, 40(2), October 2003.

Rao, Akula Rajagopala, "Socio-Economic Profile of Customers' Service in Urban Cooperative Banks: A Study", *Cooperative Perspective*, 31(2), July-September 2002.

Amin, G.H., "Need for Greater Transparency in Urban Cooperative Banks", *The Cooperator*, 41(9), 2004.

Annamalai, S., and Bhuvaneswari, P., "Urban Cooperative Banks poised for Growth", *Tamil Nadu Journal of Cooperation*, 5(11), September 2005.

Ali, Ashraf and Basavaraja Banahar, "Performance of Co-operative Oil Mills in Karnataka – A Management Appraisal", *Indian Co-operative Review*, 11(3), October 2001.

Asthana, A.K., and Manali Phatak, "Marketing of Loans/ Advances in Urban Co-operative Banks", *Agricultural Banker*, 23(1), January-March 1999.

Raikan, Avinash V., "Performance, Problems and Prospects of the Urban.

Co-operative Banks in Goa", *Indian Co-operative Review*, 42(2), October 2004.

Belay, Ayenew, Suhag, K.S., and Arun Kumar, "The Performance of Primary Agricultural Co-operative Credit Societies in Haryana", *Indian Co-operative Review*, 41(4), April 2004.

Chellani, D.K., and Rita Rai, "The Performance of District Central Cooperative Banks in Gujarat", *Indian Cooperative Review*, 41(4), April 2004.

Chidambaram, K., and Ganesan, S., "Overdues in Primary Agricultural Cooperative Banks in Madurai District: A Study", *Cooperative Perspective*, 37(3), October-December 2002.

Dash, D.K., "Financial Performance Evaluation through Ratio Analysis – A Case Study of Nawanajar Cooperative Bank", Jamnagar (Gujarat)", *Indian Cooperative Review*, 37(3), January 2000.

Dayanandan, R., and Sasikumar, K., "Performance Evaluation of District Co-operative Banks of Kerala", *Indian Co-operative Review*, 46(2), October, 2003.

Das, Debrata, "Utilisation Pattern of Cooperative Credit: A Case Study", *Cooperative Perspective*, 36(4), January-March 2002.

Bhamare, Deepak B. and Agarwal, V.S., "A Study of the Capital Structure of Dairy Co-operatives in Maharashtra: A Case Study Related to Dhule District", *The Maharashtra Co-operative Quarterly*, 83(2), October-December 1999.

Shah, Deepak, "How far Credit Co-operatives Viable in the New Economic Environment: An Evidence from Maharashtra", *Prajnan*, 30(2), 2002.

Shah, Deepak, "Primary Agricultural Co-operative Credit Societies in Maharashtra: Some Emerging Issues", *Prajnan*, 29(1), 2001.

Devara, T.S., "An Analysis of Working of District Cooperative Central Bank, Hassan Karnataka", *The Maharashtra Cooperative Quarterly*, 83(2), October-December, 1999.

Devaraja, T.S., "An Evaluation of Bee-keepers Cooperative Society Limited, Sahleshpur [Hassan District, Karnataka]", *Cooperative Perspective*, 34(1), April-June 1999.

Shah, Deepak, "Performance Evaluation of Sarada Mahila Co-operative Bank Ltd., in Mysore City of Karnataka", *The Maharashtra Co-operative Quarterly*, 84(4), April-June 2001.

Shah, Deepak, "Working of District Central Co-operative Bank, Hassan, Karnataka: An Analysis", *Indian Co-operative Review*, 35(3), January 1999.

Sen, Dilip Kumar, Sugan C. Jain and Swapan Kumar Bala, "Financial Sickness of Co-operative Organisations in Morang District", *Indian Journal of Accounting*, 33(6), December 2002.

Yadav, Dinesh Singh, "Performance and Prospects of Agricultural Cooperative Credit Societies in Block Bilhaur District Kanpur – Dehak (U.P)", *Indian Cooperative Review*, 37(2), October 1999.

Ganur, B.N., Sale, D.L., and Kale, N.K., "Performance of Cooperative Banks in Supply of Loans to the Farmers in Maharashtra", *The Maharashtra Cooperative Quarterly*, 89(4), 2003.

Goswani, H., and Hazarika, P., "Problems and Prospects of Consumer Cooperatives in Assam in the New Millennium", *Indian Cooperative Review*, 39(4), April 2002.

Gupta, R.R., "An Appraisal of the Working of Scheduled UCBs in India – Problems and Prospects", *The Cooperator*, 5(1), February 2003.

Jadhav, K.L., and Kasar, D.V., "Performance of District Central Co-operative Banks in Maharashtra: A Model for Quantitative Analysis", *The Maharashtra Co-operative Quarterly*, 101(4), January-March 2006.

Capoor, Jagadish, "Urban Cooperative Banks: Problems and Prospects", *Reserve Bank of India Bulletin*, July 2000.

Jain, P.K., "Marketing Management of Cooperative Sector", *Tamil Nadu Journal of Co-operation*, 91(2), March 2000.

Junare, S.O., "Customer Oriented Approach in Cooperative Banks", *Cooperative Perspective*, 37(1), April-June 2002.

Junare, S.O., "Role of Urban Cooperative Banks in Financing of Primity and Weaker Sector in Gujarat", National Institute of Co-operative Management, Bulletin, September 2005.

Singh, Katar, "Cooperatives Emerging Chalenges and Coping Strategies", *Kurukshetra,* November 2002.

Rao, Koteswara, M., and Chandran, K., "Performance of Consumer Cooperative Stores in Andhra Pradesh: A Case Study of Vijayakrishna Super Bazar, Vijayawada", *Indian Cooperative Review,* 42(4), April 2005.

Rao, Krishna, G.V., Chandra Shekhar and Narender, I., "Growth Analysis – A Critical Review of the Karimnagar District Cooperative Central Bank (KDCCB) Andhra Pradesh", *Indian Cooperative Review,* 38(1), July 2000.

Kulandaiswamy, V., and Murugesan, P., "Performance of PACS – An Empirical Evaluation", *Indian Co-operative Review,* 42(2), October 2004.

Lal, R.C., and Lavania, "Impact of Cooperative Credit on Agriculture Production and Income", *Indian Cooperative Review,* 23(3), 1986.

Latoria, S.K., Janlkar, A.M., and Sush, V.N., "Repayment Performance of Agricultural Credit Users in Gwaliar District (M.P)", *Land Bank Journal,* 25(1), 1998.

Latoria, S.K., Jauloar, A.M., Daipuria, O.P., and Sharma, S.K., "An Analysis of Overdues and Repayment Behaviour of Agricultural Credit (A Case Study of Gwaliar District), *Land Bank Journal,* December 2000.

Masali, S.S., "The Performance of Cooperative Urban Banks: A Study of Cooperative Urban Banks in Belgaum", *Indian Cooperative Review,* 42(1), July 2004.

Masthan, D., and Narayanasamy, R., "Financial Analysis of Chittoor Co-operative Town Bank", *Co-operative Perspective,* 35(3), October-December 2000.

Mishra, R.K., and Pattanaik, S., "Repayment Performance of Borrowers with Respect to Agricultural Loans on Khruda Block of Khunda District, Orissa", *Indian Co-operative Review,* 43(1), July 2005.

Sarangi, Mrutyunjay and Raman, M., "Discriminant Analysis of Members and Non-Members' Perception Towards Consumer Co-operatives in Tamil Nadu", *Co-operative Perspective,* 35(3), October-December 2000.

Reddy, Narasimha, S., Jayarama, ., Srinivasa, G., Lekshmana, S., and Gethadevi, R.G., "Performance of Silk Handloom Weavers' Co-operative Societies in Andhra Pradesh – A Financial Performance", *Indian Co-operative Review,* 4(2), July 1998.

Natarajan, P., and Murugesan, M., "Services of Employees Cooperative Stores – Members' Perception", *Tamil Nadu Journal of Cooperation,* 4(11), September 2004.

NSSO, "An Alternative Model for Salary Earners' Cooperative Credit Societies and Banks", *Urban Credit,* 24(1), March 2002.

Padmini, E.V.K., "Trends in Pattern of Sources and Uses of Funds of District Co-operative Banks in Kerala", *Co-operative Perspective,* 34(4), January-March 2000.

Padmini, E.V.K., and Jaish, P.C., "Financial Performance of Regional Rural Banks – A Case Study of the North Malabar Gramin Bank", *Agricultural Banker,* 23(3), July-September 1999.

Palanisamy, A., and Arunachalam, "Utilisation and Repayment of Cooperative Crop Loan", *Indian Cooperative Review,* 29(2), 1991.

Patil, K.V., "Evaluation of Financial Working and Operational Performance of Non-Agricultural Credit Societies in Jalagon District with Special Reference to Panola City", *The Maharashtra Co-operative Quarterly,* 98(1), April-June 2006.

Puhazhendhi, V., and Satysai, K.B.S., "Empowerment of Rural Women Through Self-Help Groups – An Indian Experience", *National Bank Reviews,* 18(2), April-June 2000.

Raihar, A.V., "Growth, Profitability and Cost Efficiency of Urban Co-operative Banks in India: A Comparative Analysis", *Indian Co-operative Review,* 40(2), October 2002.

Kumar, Rajitha, "Working of Urban Cooperative Banks – A Case Study", *The Maharashtra Co-operative Quarterly*, 84(4) April-June 2001.

Ramesh, D., "Restructuring of Credit Co-operatives: An Issue of Imperative Need", *The Maharashtra Co-operative Quarterly*, 97(12), January-March 2005.

Ravi Prasad, S., "Performance of Urban Co-operative Banks – Some Aspects", *The Co-operator*, 41(10), April 2004.

Rene, T., "True Productivity – The Key to Profitability", *Executive digest*, December 1991.

Rengasamy, V., "Factors Influencing Profitability of the Melur Co-operative Urban Bank An Analysis", *Tamil Nadu Journal of Co-operation*, 1(8), June 2001.

Lopoyelum, Samwel Kakuko, "A Micro-analysis of the Cost of Default and Evaluation of Primary Agricultural Co-operative Banks (PACBs) – A Case of Rural Financing", *Co-operative Perspective*, 35(3), October-December 2000.

Sarhar, A.N., "Problems and Prospects of Weavers' Co-operative Societies in Maharashtra", *Co-operative Perspective*, 37(2), July-September 2002.

Satish, P., and Desh Pande, D.V., "Co-operative Banks and Regional Rural Banks: The Challenges Ahead,_Agricultural Banker, 23(3), July-September 1999.

Satyanarayana, G.S., "Challenges Before Scheduled and Large UCBs in the New Millennium", *Urban Credit*, 21(4), 1999.

Shah, Deepak, "Co-operative Dairying in Maharashtra: Lessons to be Learned", *Economic and Political Weekly*, 32(39), September 1997.

Shankaran, P.N., "Performance of Primary Cooperative Agricultural Development Banks in Kerala: A Model for Quantitative Analysis", *Indian Cooperative Review*, 33(1), 1995.

Sharma, S.K., Daipura, O.P., Janlkar, A.M., and Latoria, S.K., "An Analysis of Overdues and Repayment Behaviour of Agricultural Credit", *Land Bank Journal*, December 2000.

Singh, Padam and Rattan Chand, "Quality of Live Approach for Identification of Poor", *Journal of Rural Development*, 19(1), 2000.

Singh, S.K., Singh, R.I., and Singh, G.N., "Impact of rural Cooperative Credit on Agricultural Development in Eastern UP", *Indian Cooperative Review*, 27(1), 1989.

Sivaprahasam, P., "Working of the Employees Cooperative Credit Societies in Tamil Nadu", *Tamil Nadu Journal of Cooperation*, 91(10), January 2000.

Bhattacharjee, Sourindra, "Factors Influencing Viability of Primary Agricultural Co-operative Credit Societies", *Prajnan*, 27(1), 1999.

Nayak, Sri Sudarsan, "Cooperative – The Vehicle of Economic Growth with Specific reference to Orissa", *Indian Cooperative Review*, 42(1), July 2004.

Srinath, A.R., "Co-operative Credit in India – Problems and Suggestions", *Indian Consumer Co-operator*, 28 (2), April-June 2001.

Subbiah, A., "Deposits, Loans issued on Recovery Performance of Central Cooperative Banks in India", *Tamil Nadu Journal of Cooperation*, 91(6), September 1999.

Subburaj, B., and Karunakaran, P., "Adoption of Modern Strategies by Urban Co-operative Banks in Tamil Nadu", *Indian Co-operative Review*, 29(3), January 2002.

Suhag, K.S., Goyal, S.K., and Grora, R.K., "The Performance of Co-operative Credit Institutions in Haryana", *Indian Co-operative Review*, 35(4), April 1998.

Suhag, K.S., Parminder Malik and Arun Kumar, "Performance of Primary Agricultural Co-operative Credit Societies in Haryana", *Indian Economic Panorama*, 15(2), July 2005.

Sukhdev Singh and Maninder Kaur, "Performance of Agricultural Cooperative Service Societies in Punjab: An Appraisal", *Cooperative Perspective*, 34(4), January-March 2000.

Taori, V.K., "An Analytical View on Urban Cooperative Banks", *The Cooperatives,* 42(10), April 2005.

Teli, R.B., "An Evaluation of the Working of Urban Cooperative Banking in India – Problems and Prospects", *Indian Cooperative Review,* 42(1), July 2004.

Teli, R.B., "Performance Evaluation of Urban Co-operative Banks in Kolhapur District", *The Maharashtra Co-operative Quarterly,* 98(1), April-June 2006.

Teli, R.B., "Performance Evaluation of Urban Co-operative Banks in Kolhapur District", *Indian Co-operative Review,* 43(1), July 2005.

Thiripurasundari, K., "Problems of Overdues in Co-operative Housing Societies – A Case Study", *Indian Co-operative Review,* 41(1), July 2003.

Thiripurasundari, K, "Problems of the Co-operative Housing Societies – A Case Analysis", *The Co-operator,* 43(7), January 2006.

Thiruthuvadoss, S.P., "Determinants of Profit in District Central Cooperative Banks", *Tamil Nadu Journal of Cooperation,* 4(5), March 2004.

Varkey, V.O., "An Urban Credit Society's Progress and Training Outlook", *The Maharashtra Co-operative Quarterly,* 80(4), January-March 1996.

Veera Kumaran, G., and Subash, B., "The Palakkad Urban Co-operative Bank Limited – A Case Study", *Indian Co-operative Review,* 37(4), April 2001.

Vimala, P., "Customer Service in Cooperatives", *Indian Co-operative Review,* 41(4), April 2004.

Zahir Hussain, A.K., "Malabar's Pride: Performance Evaluation of the Malappuram District Central Cooperative Bank Ltd.", *Cooperative Perspective,* 38(2), July-September 2003.

Zahir Hussain, A.K., "Problems and Prospects of Service Cooperative Banks in Kerala", *Tamil Nadu Journal of Cooperation,* 5(7), May 2005.

Zahir Hussain, A.K., "Status of Service Co-operative Banks in Kerala", *The Co-operator*, 42(11), May 2005.

REPORTS

Audit Reports of Individual Employees Co-operative Thrift and Credit Societies of Kanyakumari District from 1994-1995 to 2003-2004.

Report of the Central Banking Committee, 1931, Vol.1, Part 1.

Sahayoga, "The Role of Cooperative in Reducing Regional Imbalances in Karnataka", Report submitted to the High Power Committee for Redressal of Regional Imbalances, Government of Karnataka, June 2002.

Index

❑❑❑